THE POWER OF IMPERFECT PARENTS

Practical tools to parent your child with disabilities

THE POWER OF IMPERFECT PARENTS

Practical tools to parent your child with disabilities

Lynda Drake

The Power of Imperfect Parents: Practical Tools to Parent Your Child with Disabilities
Copyright © 2023 by Lynda Drake

Published in the United States of America
ISBN   Paperback: 978-1-960629-93-7
ISBN   Hardback: 978-1-960629-95-1
ISBN   eBook: 978-1-960629-94-4

All rights reserved. No part of this publication may be reproduced, stored in a retrieval system or transmitted in any way by any means, electronic, mechanical, photocopy, recording or otherwise without the prior permission of the author except as provided by USA copyright law.

The opinions expressed by the author are not necessarily those of ReadersMagnet, LLC.

ReadersMagnet, LLC
10620 Treena Street, Suite 230 | San Diego, California, 92131 USA
1.619. 354. 2643 | www.readersmagnet.com

Book design copyright © 2023 by ReadersMagnet, LLC. All rights reserved.

Cover design by Ericka Obando
Interior design by Don De Guzman

This book is dedicated to my parents, grandparents, husband, and children, who have taught me about parenting, love, acceptance, and inclusion.

CONTENTS

Forward 1
Introduction; Why Not Me? 3

1. Expectations In Holland 7
2. Unconditional Love 14
3. Letting Go 18
4. The Importance Of Disappointment And Failure 26
5. Help And Support 30
6. Doctors And Other Professionals 36
7. Food's New Meaning 43
8. Become Your Child's Advocate 49
9. Discipline And Employment 54
10. Friends Are A Precious Commodity 63
11. Siblings, The Great Balancing Act 67
12. Money Matters 70
13. Behaviors, Now What? 73
14. The Importance Of Sexuality 79
15. Humor! A Survival Tool 83
16. Spiritual Life 86
17. Precious Time 89
18. Self And Relationship Care 92
19. Disability Specific Information 96
20. The Big Reveal 103

About The Author 121
About The Original Cover Artist 122
Sayings For Life 123

FORWARD

By David Henninger

The title of this book, *The Power of Imperfect Parents,* might surprise a few readers. It contains two words, 'power' and 'imperfect' that might be perceived as contradictory. The goal of many of us is to be a 'perfect' parent and the word 'power' might mean total control.

The reader does not have to read too far into this book to begin understanding that the title is aptly named. Through very candid lens, the author, Lynda Drake, has shared her direct experience of parenting her three children, each of whom has dealt with challenges that can be labeled as disabilities. Seldom are we able to share the experience of having a parent detail the ups and downs of living in an uncharted world where each child has a different disability that presents its own set of unique challenges to parents and the siblings involved.

As someone who has had the honor of working for Bayaud Enterprises and having an office that adjoins hers, I can attest that Ms. Drake is the 'real deal.' When you read her book, you will see that the person who has written it is sharing real life trial-and-error experiences that offer life affirming lessons that all of us can incorporate into our lives.

The word 'love' is used so commonly that it is easy to brush it aside as a cliché. But, in this book, the genuine power of 'love' comes through time and time again. The intimate look inside the dynamics of a family facing all of the trials/tribulations of parenting have seldom been expressed so openly. Any person who has been the parent of an individual with a disability will be able to gain new insight and practical tips to make the journey feel less lonely.

By adding the interviews of other individuals who live with a disability and what they felt were the important factors in their own parents that did or didn't work for them, Ms. Drake informs us even more about the vital role parents play in the raising of children who have a disability. This book is not just for parents who have a child with a disability, but for all people who have interactions with those who are living the experience of parenting.

Indeed, when the reader finishes this book, the title makes 'perfect' sense.

David Henninger
Executive Director of Bayaud Enterprises

INTRODUCTION; WHY NOT ME?

Many people who write books ask themselves, "Why me? Am I worthy to share this story or information?" When the book is about parenting, which has a way of making all of us doubt ourselves, especially when it's parenting children with special challenges, I really questioned myself.

I will admit I am an imperfect parent. Indeed 'perfect parent' is an oxymoron. There is no way to be a perfect parent; there are too many variables with each one being a judgment call without a definitive, perfect answer. I decided to change the question to, "Why not me?" I believe that the experiences I have been through, my willingness to be authentic and show you all who I am, my vulnerabilities, my failures, and my strengths, just might guide you on your own path — give you a tool that may illuminate your path, show you that you can do this and remind you that you can be the parent you hoped you would be.

There have been times when parenting my children has felt like it was too difficult. There was too much to do and too little time, too little of me. Being a working mother is one of the hardest jobs you can do. I have worked for most of my children's lives except for about three years when they were babies becoming toddlers. I worked in the stock brokerage business until our oldest daughter, Alli, was 13, and our twins, Alex and Katy, were 6 years old. In this field, punctuality is critical, and being at work every day, mandatory. Their father, my husband Fred, was a printer during this time. It was also imperative that he was at work and on time. This was challenging because Alex has Down syndrome, at that point his only diagnosis. His sister, Alli, had been diagnosed with ADD and dyslexia, but his twin sister had not been labeled with anything yet.

I felt like a failure everywhere. I felt like a failure at work because of the time I had to miss it because one of the kids was sick or Alex had therapy or other treatments that were required. I felt like a failure as a mother because I couldn't be with my children as much as they needed me.

It was at this time when our kids were 6 and 13, I was finally able to quit my job at Schwab and work from home. This was not a good financial decision, (we ended up filing bankruptcy eight years later), but it was a much better decision for my spiritual and emotional well-being. We were fortunate that I had that option available. I was only able to work from home for two years before going back into the workforce in a completely different field as a job developer, helping people with disabilities find jobs. This was a job that I had felt called to do many years before (more about that in the chapter on employment), and I was grateful for the opportunity to try it.

As the years rolled on, each of my children picked up new diagnoses. For Alex, he added type 1 diabetes, autism, sleep apnea, and anxiety/mood disorder. And in high school, Katy discovered she had severe, life-threatening allergies to almost all types of fish, shellfish and marijuana, as well as pain issues in her back and other places. Life got more complicated. In the times when it felt too hard, some angel would tell me I was doing a great job as a mom. That would help me see that maybe they were right even if I didn't feel that way. Maybe I could do this parenting thing. I'm grateful my husband and I did it and are still doing it together. We know how lucky we are to have remained life partners, co-caregivers, and best friends. Not always easy.

These days, our children are older but that doesn't mean they need us less. Alex requires constant care. We are fortunate that Fred is now paid to stay home with him through a program called CDASS which stands for Consumer Directed Attendant Support Services, pronounced c-dass. This program allows us to choose who should be paid to care for our son.

I work for a non-profit agency called Bayaud Enterprises which assists people with disabilities and those experiencing homelessness find work. I am a job developer, program manager, group facilitator, and speaker for them. As a job developer, I have assisted over 1000 individuals with various challenges find jobs and the tools they need to achieve whatever success means to them.

There is a chapter in this book that will show you how to guide your child to be more employable. I have learned a great deal during the past 20 years about what it takes to be successful in the workplace and the qualities employers look for in employees. I hope these tips can assist with preparing your child for employment in the future. Having a job can be life-changing for individuals with disabilities, as it can for all of us. The way we parent them can make a huge difference in whether that is possible.

In this book, in addition to talking about employment, we will also go over how to change our expectations, not only about what our children will accomplish in life, but how our lives will change. If we allow it, most of the changes can be positive and all of the changes hold amazing lessons for us. One of the greatest lessons we learn from our kids is unconditional love which we will talk about.

There is a chapter on how to teach our children the importance of disappointment and failure, how to deal with doctors and other professionals, how to keep food a positive experience and how to balance our attention between all our children.

We will discuss important topics regarding friendships, how to talk to our children about sex and money, and what they teach us about spirituality. There is a chapter on how to handle severe behaviors, how to practice self and relationship care and information about various disabilities, including Down syndrome, ADD, allergies, mood disorder, type 1 diabetes, and more.

This book will remind us that all our children are amazing people who each have their own challenges and gifts. Our children become who they are not only because of the parenting they receive, but also their siblings, grandparents, environment, experiences in life and, of course, genes. We can't control everything but we can continue to improve how we show up as parents. Give yourself credit for the skills you have even as you strive to do better. It doesn't serve anyone to beat yourself up.

In our society, there is the expectation that you will be a 'perfect' parent. We have been told the importance of raising healthy kids who dress well, are clean, good looking, maintain a healthy weight, are smart, participate in sports, and on and on. But the truth is every child is different and has their own unique way of being themselves. In this book, we will explore more about parenting to the best of our ability. Being able to see the gifts and lessons has helped me to embrace the power that comes with allowing ourselves to be imperfect parents. I am learning to change my focus to be a loving parent who finds the lessons of life, learns to laugh, and let go of what no longer serves me.

For those times when you feel overwhelmed, allow that to be how you feel. Accept it. Accept yourself just as you are. Love yourself just as you are. Then you will be able to release that emotion sooner instead of stuffing it down into your soul and pretending you can do it all. Ask for help. Take a moment; everything doesn't have to be solved in this moment. As a matter of fact, it is impossible to solve everything right now.

Bite off what you can when you can; deal with that bite and then move on to the next. Take breaks or talk to someone about what is going on in between bites so you can more effectively deal with the chewing of that bite before moving on to the next. Do what you can and don't beat yourself up. If you are having a really hard time with some bite, ask for help. It is not a sign of weakness but rather an opportunity for grace. When we allow someone into our challenges and allow them to hold our hands while we deal with the situation, we also allow them to have grace in that moment. We learn as parents of our special kids that it is a beautiful thing when we allow people to give and allow ourselves to receive.

Life Bites at the end of each chapter give you the most important 'Bites' of information covered in the chapter for you to 'chew' on. There are some new ideas presented in this book. You may not agree with everything and that's okay. My hope is that this book will guide you to look at things in a new way and give you tools to deal with the challenges ahead. We will learn to look at ourselves and our lives through the lens of laughter, lessons, love, and letting go, so that you and your children become who you are meant to be and realize you are not alone, *ever*!

EXPECTATIONS IN HOLLAND

After Alex was born, we received a packet of information from Pilot Parents (which is a support group of parents in Omaha, Nebraska, who have children with all types of disabilities). Inside the packet was this essay called, "Welcome to Holland" by Emily Perl Kingsley, a woman who has a son with Down syndrome. In it, she compares having a child with special needs to planning a trip to Italy. You prepare for it, you plan where you will go, you learn some phrases in Italian, and then the big day arrives. You get on the plane and when it lands, they announce, "Welcome to Holland!" Expectations change.

You are disappointed; you had planned for Italy after all. Your friends all went to Italy. Then you realize you have a choice: whether to let go of the expectation of Italy and decide to see the beauty of Holland or to stay in that place of grief and disappointment. I'm grateful that my husband and I didn't take too long to choose to find the beauty of Holland, even though there are still occasions when we are sad we didn't get to Italy. There is grief when you have a child born with a disability. You must grieve the passing of the child you expected so that you can truly celebrate the one you received.

If you are like me, there have been many moments when you have felt inadequate at this important job of raising a special needs child. But, trust me, you're not! You can do this, not alone, reaching out for help when you need to, but in the end, you will rise to the challenge and reap the rewards. Our rewards don't often come in the big events, like college graduation. They come in the beautiful small moments; the first time your child says "I love you" or hugs you or goes to the bathroom in the toilet or tries broccoli or runs the right way on the soccer field. These moments can be wonderful and what keep us going.

In order to enjoy these moments, we sometimes have to change the expectations we had when we were expecting a 'typical' child. Before my children were born, I expected them to be able to drive a car one day, go to prom and college, get married, have children and a job. Sometimes that expectation changes at birth when the child is born with a disability and sometimes it changes as they grow and develop a new diagnosis. For my own family I have had to let go of expectations involving relationships, marriage, and the possibility of having children. Alli having ADD and dyslexia has created challenges in relationships, jobs, and completing college. Because of Katy's life-threatening allergies, jobs and living situations can be dangerous. Alex's developmental disability means that many expectations are in question. It isn't that these experiences are impossible; they just have extra challenges and may require additional work to achieve.

For Alli, I let go of the idea that school would be easy. I had to change my approach when helping her with her homework, especially math homework. With assistance from professionals, I learned that Alli thinks visually, so the more I could show something, the more it helped her. Like for subtraction in math, I show an apple pie and then take away some of the pieces. In the case of division, I used examples like, if you have four dogs and five cups of dog food, how much food will you be able to give each dog?

Alli went to college for a couple years. One of her professors said she was the hardest-working student he had ever had. But it wasn't something that was important enough to her to finish. My expectation had to change and I accepted her decision. It has worked out fine for her. She has a great job that she loves with an ambulance company and she has no student loans.

As Katy grew and developed various diagnoses, I had to let go of the expectation that she would be healthy. I had to accept the fact that there would be days when she didn't feel well and times when severe allergic reactions would send her to the emergency room or hospital.

She discovered her severe allergy to marijuana after attempting to go to college in Boulder, Colorado. She was exposed to marijuana one night. Since she had already had numerous allergic reactions, she knew what was happening and to get out of the apartment, call us, and go to the emergency room. This allergy made completing college a challenge, but through a great deal of hard work and four colleges, she was able to graduate. Her last semester, she went to school at a university in Denver through skype and the wonder of online technology, even though she was living in Muncie, Indiana at the time. Denver had legalized marijuana which made a college campus there unsafe. The fact that she went to college had been an expectation for me, but it had to be one *she* wanted badly enough to put in the work necessary to graduate. She even went on to get her Master's Degree in Social Work.

I also had to let go of the expectation that she would live in Colorado since there was just too much pot. This was a hard expectation to release. I didn't know how I would cope with having a child live so far away. But it has worked out and there are good things about her living far away. Because we don't see each other all the time, we make sure to focus on the quality of time when we are together. This has been hardest on Alex, but he is adjusting well and really loves to see her when he gets the chance.

For Alex, I let go of many expectations, but one of the expectations I couldn't let go of, was prom. He loves to dance, especially with pretty, young ladies and loves to be social on his own terms. It would have been too sad to not make that happen. But there was no way he would make it at his high school. He had already been kicked out of there as a freshman because of his behavior and was now going to a school for kids with emotional issues or dual diagnosis. This is when you have more than one diagnosis, like for Alex he is developmentally delayed, on the autism spectrum, and has mental health issues.

This school was quite small with a total of about 40 students, and they did not offer prom. Katy and I decided to take matters into our own hands and create one ourselves. We called it Prom for All. We had it at a local hotel ballroom, we invited people with disabilities from all over, and we recruited volunteers from Katy's high school. It was a great success! We had about 30 people with disabilities attend and about that same number of 'typical' volunteers. Everyone got all dressed up and came ready to dance. Alex had a blast! It was such a success we did it for three more years.

Some expectations we must release and replace with an alternative to the old 'normal'. This new 'normal' will open up the possibilities of your child's capabilities, giving you the opportunity to embrace them. We, in the meantime, work on the delicate balancing act of expecting the best from our children while being realistic about their abilities and limitations and what we can do to create places for them to thrive — trying as often as possible to let them do all that they can by themselves. When we allow our children to do things, like chores around the house, or putting on their own clothes and shoes, we must be ready to give them the time and space to do it. Alex will empty the dishwasher, but you may have to leave it open all day for him to get it done.

All my kids put on their own clothes, but there were times when they were quite creative in their fashion sense. When Katy was about four years old, she would wear this beautiful pink taffeta dress with a full petticoat that made the skirt stand out. She wore it almost every day, including sleeping in it! It wasn't what I would choose. But that's okay as long as it's safe. We do have to make sure they aren't putting on shorts and flip flops if it is below zero outside. But if it is just a bit mismatched, so what? No one has ever died from wearing plaid pants and a shirt full of flowers. We need to give them space for their own self-expression. You may not be able to do this every time, but make sure to give them the time and space to do as much for themselves as they can.

When our son, Alex, was about 12 years old, I had him wash his own laundry. He loved putting the soap in, throwing the clothes in, and turning on the washer. Did he look for stains? Not a chance! Did he separate whites and darks? Dream on! But everything got relatively clean and he felt good about doing it. That lasted until he was about 14, but then life got crazier; he got more resistant to listening and we stopped expecting him to do it. It's on my list of things to try again someday.

One of my struggles is when I see other children doing things I wish my child could do, like reading (which was a challenge for all of our children, as it was for Fred and me). Another challenge is not to compare your kids to others, and it's difficult for them not to compare themselves to their peers. It's hard not to compare your child to others with the same disability who might be 'higher functioning' than your child. This is still a challenge for me at times.

When I see what other people with Down syndrome can do that Alex can't do, I question if it was because of my parenting abilities. Intellectually, I know that is probably not the case, but it can still be a hard sell to my heart. It doesn't serve us or our children to stay in the place of beating ourselves up as parents. When I am in those moments, I try to be grateful for all the other children can do and grateful for all that my child can do, and let it go.

Alex went to a transition school (which is a public school for young people with disabilities aged 18 to 21), with Megan Bomgaars from the television show "Born This Way." She is an amazing young lady with a great mom. I can try to compare Alex to Megan as far as what they can do, but that wouldn't get me very far. It seems to be much more productive to congratulate Megan and her mom on a job well done. Her mother has given Megan the opportunity to grow and take risks. Together, they have pushed the envelope as far as the expectations for people with Down syndrome. Who knows how that will open more doors for others with disabilities? For that, and all that Megan will do in her life, I am grateful.

Another expectation we have as parents is that one day our child will move out of the house. This is not a certainty for children with many types of disabilities, or any child for that matter. There are some group or host homes that your adult child may have access to, but there are often long wait lists for them. A group home is where staff operate the home 24/7, but they do not necessarily live there. A host home is where a small group of individuals with disabilities (or perhaps only one), live with a person, couple, or family who are paid for this service.

We decided as a family that Alex would stay with us as long as possible. There are positives and negatives to that decision. The positive is that Fred is paid to stay home with Alex, which has worked out well. Alex loves to stay home and do things on his time, as opposed to going to a day program. Day programs can be good, especially if your child is social, but for Alex it just wasn't a good fit. It wasn't a good fit for him because he had such a difficult time being convinced to go every morning. It could sometimes take over an hour to get him out of the house and into the car. We tried bribing him with a surprise in the car or telling him that if he went, his grandma would pick him up. There were times that it would trigger a behavior where he would throw things and try to hurt us, which would end in us calling the police to help get him calmed down.

It got to be too much for us as a family, so when Fred was able to stay home with him, it was really life-changing for us. The challenge with him staying home is that it can be difficult for him to go out at all. Fred is learning what does motivate him to leave, like going to movies that he likes early in the morning when there aren't many people there or going swimming or to play basketball.

A possible benefit to living in a group or host home is that they may have access to more activities and more interactions with people who are not family. One of the other good things is that when the parents can no longer take care of the child, they are already used to living with someone else so there aren't as many changes at one time, which can be very traumatic.

Learning what is best for your child takes listening to the child, everyone in the family, and maybe some interested professionals or friends. There are many things to think about and these are decisions that make a big impact on everyone, so do it carefully and take the time to really think about it.

Emily Perl Kingsley, the author of the 'Welcome to Holland' poem, has these words of wisdom:

"I would also add that although Jason's (her son with Down syndrome) accomplishments were pretty impressive (starting to read at an early age, acting on television, writing a book, etc.), all of that is not important at all and should *never* be seen as a yardstick against which you should ever measure or compare your own child.

The *only* thing that is important is that your child should be encouraged to do whatever *your* child is capable of. Your child should be educated and stimulated to learn and grow and realize whatever is YOUR child's potential! Celebrate and enjoy all the development and all the achievements your child accomplishes. That is the only thing that counts! The more fun you have with your child, the better!"

Thank you, Emily, for reminding us of what is really important in this whole parenting thing!

LIFE BITES:

- Keep an open heart so that you can let go of expectations that don't fit your child and be open to the gift that is your child.
- Remember to balance expecting the best out of your child while being realistic about their abilities.
- Create places for them to thrive.
- Give them time and space to allow them to try and achieve what they can while giving them permission to fail.

UNCONDITIONAL LOVE

The greatest gift I believe our special needs children give us is love. Real, unconditional love. My children have shown me how to feel love and empathy without judgement.

Alli taught me about loving the underdog, about generosity and compassion. She can feel how others are feeling. This has guided her actions with compassion and empathy. She feels what others are needing and reaches out to them with generosity, giving what she has to them if they need it. She has always been able to feel when I am at the end of my rope and steps in to help — like when I was tired, and the twins were needing a lot of attention. She would offer to play with them for a little so I could get some rest.

Katy, who, because of her life-threatening allergies understands how precious life is, taught me to always say *I love you* when we end a conversation because you never know when it will be your last chance. It was a powerful reminder that family is more important than my job. All the times that she was rushed to the emergency room due to anaphylaxis (which is a severe allergic reaction that can restrict breathing and if untreated, it can lead to death), I felt fear — the fear of losing something that I loved so much, the type of fear that brought me to my knees and to God's doorway where I surrendered to the power of the universe, where I learned to let love lead me in my life.

Alex taught me to love without holding back — to love the stranger or friend or neighbor or grandma and to love them completely. One time, Alex had a doctor who had not been nice to him. The first thing the doctor said to Alex was, "He's so obese." That didn't faze Alex one bit. When we were finished with the appointment, Alex gave the doctor a big hug and said, "I love you!" The doctor was obviously shocked and said, "You are one of the few."

All throughout Alex's childhood until he was about 17, he would say with a smile on his face in great anticipation for a new day, "Happy day!" Through his challenges, he can always find a reason to be happy. His speech is so difficult to understand that there are times even his family can't understand it. I can't imagine how challenging that would be. But he keeps going with a positive attitude, at least most of the time. Alex has taught me how to love my inner child and to play. With Alex, my inner child and I get to swim for fun, go to kids' movies, and laugh or cry, and dance in my living room. I feel such joy in these moments. When Alex is having a behavior episode, I have learned to work my love muscle and hold a space of love even when it is difficult.

What a great reminder of the power of love and what is important in life! My kids get love, they understand it, and have taught me about it. What a great gift, one of the many of having special kids!

As we guide our children to be their best selves, remember to keep love as your guide. Sometimes when we look at our children, all we see is the 'disability.' From this viewpoint, we can parent them from a place of feeling sorry for them instead of loving them. Remember feeling sorry for someone is also judging them, and when we are judging someone, we can't be truly loving them. There will be moments when we are sorry for what they must go through, like when they don't get invited to a birthday party, or they are teased or mistreated, or are physically sick and hurting. Allow yourself to feel that, but then move through it. Don't get stuck and parent from there.

If you parent from a place of pity, you won't expect much from your child; you won't give them the opportunity to do the things they are capable of doing. You will be afraid to let them fail, get disappointed or hurt. But it is when all of us fail, get disappointed, and hurt that we learn the life lessons that help us be adults with hopeful expectations and healthy relationships which are so important in a happy life. It seems like our kids would be happy if they never felt disappointment, but that isn't how life works. Show them that you love and respect them enough to know that they can grow through life's setbacks to become strong, emotionally healthy, loving adults.

When we step back in our lives to see the big picture, instead of just the little puzzle pieces that make up the pictures of life, it can guide us to see through a lens of love and lesson — what we are here to learn. There is a Buddhist quote that says, "If you focus on the hurt, you will continue to suffer. If you focus on the lesson, you will continue to grow."

We didn't know that Alex had Down syndrome until he and Katy were born. When the doctor told us, "Your son has Down syndrome," I was shocked. I didn't know what to feel. My first thought was, "He's Mongoloid?" which was a derogatory term used to describe people who had Down syndrome and one that I had heard in my life more than the term Down syndrome.

That was a puzzle piece I wasn't expecting. I really didn't know much about it at all. I had only known one other person who had Down syndrome and I didn't know him well. I had no idea how it would affect our family and our lives. I had many questions and concerns. But I did know with love and support I would get through it and that it would be a valuable lesson. As I grew to accept the diagnosis, I knew I couldn't fix it, or cure it, but through herbs and other treatments, I could make it the mildest case of Down syndrome ever. I think many of us parents do that. We are no longer in total denial, but we are also not completely accepting everything about our children, I know I wasn't.

When he was about four years old, in 1997, I went to a past life regression class with a friend from work. At the time I didn't believe in past lives and I'm not here to prove or disprove reincarnation now. Instead of asking yourself if you believe or don't believe in past lives, try changing the question to, "What if we do live more than one life? How would that change my experience of this life? Is there value in this thought?"

In the class, the person hypnotized us as we lay on the floor, similar to a meditation. The hypnotist walked us back further and further in time. I got a vision of a woman standing in a kitchen in what appeared to be the mid 1800's. Next to her was a little red-headed boy. I realized that it was Alex and I in different bodies. I got an overwhelming feeling or *knowing* that Alex had fought in that life in the Civil War and had come to this life with Down syndrome so he would never have to fight in another war. Talk about instantly allowing me to see the entire picture instead of just a puzzle piece! I could suddenly see Down syndrome for what it was; it was perfect.

Down syndrome also allowed my family to learn many lessons from Alex, like the lesson of unconditional love, patience, compassion, and staying in touch with our inner child. Looking at the big picture allows us to see the lessons we are here to learn and find the love. What a great gift!

LIFE BITES:

- Keep love as your guide.
- Don't parent from a place of pity.
- Remember that we learn the most through our challenges and failures in life. Bless the challenge and focus on the solution.
- Step back so you can see the big picture of your life and not just the puzzle pieces.
- "If you focus on the hurt, you will continue to suffer; if you focus on the lesson you will continue to grow." Buddhist quote

LETTING GO

We have talked a little about letting go of expectations for our children, but we can also let go of our perfection. Before our twins were born, I was a stockbroker for Charles Schwab. My husband and I were young; we worked hard, had great jobs, could pay our bills, went to work, came home, and complained about those great jobs. We didn't need help from anyone; we were perfect. We were living the American dream! But then we had three little bundles that taught us reality, humility, and grace. Having children with labels can do that to us; they can teach us the value of letting go, especially letting go of our expectations to be perfect.

Suddenly, my life of perfection had to take a dose of reality. My husband and I could *not* do this alone! We needed the help of family and friends, sometimes even strangers. For a few of our friends, the fact that we had a special needs child was difficult. They might not have known what to say or do, so they said or did nothing. There were a couple of people who had been a part of our lives whom we never heard from again. I had to let go of the anger or hurt I felt toward them. People are often afraid of what they don't know. Maybe they will come around some day and maybe they won't; the truth is, either way, that is okay. I have chosen to walk the path of this life with my mind and heart open. I have learned to accept each day as it is and work on moving forward.

I had to let go of always having a perfectly neat house and children who were perfectly cleaned and dressed. (although my mother-in-law would say it was never something I had!) I had to let people see me and my house when we were a mess. I let go of the façade of perfection and you know what? People understood and loved me through the mess!

You may not have as many friends as you had before all this began, but the friends that are left are real. The life that you lead now is real —

with real expectations of doing what you can each day and leaving what can't get done until tomorrow, or the next day or the next day until you realize it must not be that important after all.

There are things in our children's lives that we can't control. How we react to these situations and our attitude about it is where our power lies. One of the situations that is challenging to deal with is when our child is in a relationship that appears toxic or unhealthy. When Alli was 18 years old, she met and began dating an older man (he was 32 at the time). Fred and I were not excited by this idea, but we met him and allowed the relationship to continue. I say 'allowed' as if we really had control over what our adult child did. We might have been able to give her some words of wisdom to discourage it, but in the end, it was up to her. A year later, they moved in together. I didn't blame her for wanting to move out; living in our house could be pretty intense sometimes!

She lived with him for nine years. During this time, we didn't see her often, usually just for holidays and birthdays. For the last two years of the relationship, I went to their apartment every month just to see how things were going and to spend some time together. But I didn't realize how toxic this relationship was until she finally left him and moved back in with us. That is when I found out that she was a cutter. A cutter is someone who cuts her skin so that she feels physical pain because the emotional pain she is going through is too much to bear. This was hard for me to accept. I felt like such a failure! Why hadn't I noticed this? How could I have let it happen? Why did I let her stay with him so long?

It was a huge challenge for her to stop cutting herself. She started to heal when she became involved with the Wiccan religion because one of their main rules is *harm none*, and she realized that included herself. She got a tattoo on her wrist to remind her and she discovered it was good to discipline herself by not allowing the cutting to go on. Now when she feels like cutting, she will put on a Band-Aid to remind her that healing is more important and that she is worth healing.

Alli also believes that if there is a person in your life who makes you feel like cutting yourself, don't keep him in your life because you are worth more than that. If this person is a family member that you feel you can't leave, you may need professional help like counseling to teach you how to deal with that person in a more effective way. I do not believe that just because we are family, we must stay together no matter what. If someone is always hurting you, at least find ways to reduce how often you must spend time with them. Learn to let go.

From the time Katy was 13 years old until she was about 20, every time my cell phone would ring, and I would see it was her calling, my heart would sink, and I would feel a sense of dread. This is because about 70% of the time she was calling was because of another severe allergic reaction that would probably require an emergency room visit. I would get that nasty feeling in the pit of my stomach wondering if she would be okay — followed by an almost equally nasty feeling of how much is that going to cost? It is a terrible feeling to be almost as worried about the cost of my child's health care as I am about the outcome of the medical visit. During those years, our out-of-pocket medical costs were $10,000 to $15,000 per year. I had to learn how to let go of all that worry!

Worry only serves a purpose if we use it to find solutions and then let it go and move on. The solutions this worry led us to, was finding a service dog for Katy that would smell what she was allergic to so she could avoid the allergen. This dog, Justice, was life-changing for Katy, reducing her emergency room visits from at least once a month to about one or two times a year. He also helped her deal with the anxiety associated with having such severe allergies. Katy once described this anxiety to me. She said it is like knowing the people around you could have a loaded gun that they might shoot you with at any minute. Justice helped her let go of that anxiety and helped me let go of my worry. For those times when I still feel that feeling in the pit of my stomach, I now send blessings instead.

Sending blessings is a great way to release our fear, change the energy of the situation to love, and surrender the outcome to the universe. Sometimes it is hard to believe, but the universe, or God, or life, whatever you want to call it, always has our back and things are always working out for us.

In my job of 22 years helping people with disabilities find work, I have heard stories that demonstrate that things work out for the best when we release fear and allow things to work out as they will. Here are some of those stories:

A woman at 40 years old became legally blind overnight. After she was able to accept what had happened and discover how to love herself just as she was, she has gone on to get her Master's Degree in Vocational Rehabilitation, travel the world, start her own business, and marry the man of her dreams.

Another woman, during her last year in nursing school, had a stroke that left her in a coma for 6 weeks. Through her own determination, she has regained most of her cognition. She has partial paralysis on one side which requires her to use a wheelchair. She now says that before her stroke, she wasn't really living. Now she is working, she has a YouTube channel, she is an avid gardener, and she won Miss Wheelchair Colorado.

A man, who at the age of five, had a brain tumor removed from his brain that caused him to be blind. About a year after becoming blind, he learned braille and was given the Bible in braille. He read the Bible verse John 9:1-3 which is talking about a man who had been blind since birth. Jesus was asked who had sinned that made the child be born blind. Jesus answered, "Neither hath this man sinned, nor his parents: but that the works of God should be made manifest in him." He decided to live his life following this scripture; he has been an inspiration to many. He is also a songwriter and singer.

Of course, everyone who goes through trauma does not turn it into a triumph. It takes loving yourself, having people who believe in you and walk beside you to empower you instead of doing everything for you and pitying you. It is not an easy road to turn trauma into triumph, not for the person who has been through the trauma or the one loving them on their journey. But reminding yourself that the universe always has your back and things are always working out for you can help empower you through the process. Something else that I have used to help me to find strength when I or someone I care about is going through challenging times is to send blessings, as I mentioned earlier.

I learned about sending blessings from a great book which I highly recommend; it is by Pierre Pradervand called, *The Gentle Art of Blessing*. This book was life-changing for me. When I am worried about Katy, I send a blessing of love followed by a blessing that whatever happens will be in her highest good. I also send a blessing of abundance well used and that we always have enough to pay for what we need. We have since paid off all those medical bills, some of them through bankruptcy. I lived through it and learned to let go.

A blessing is different from a prayer. When you pray, you are asking a Higher Power to do something. For instance, "Dear God, please heal my child." With a blessing, you are taking the beautiful energy of the universe and sending it through you to the other person or situation. For example, "I send you blessings of healing energy flowing through you, blessings to the doctors and nurses helping you heal that they are in their right job, blessings of gratitude for their courage, wisdom and healing ability."

It is very powerful. It is the most powerful when you send a blessing to someone who you believe has done something 'wrong' or something that brings up anger for you. For instance, I recently had my credit card stolen and used for over $1200 of purchases. I sent the person a blessing that they see themselves as the perfect expression of Source/God, completely loved by the universe, that they live in integrity and are in their right jobs. Make sure when sending a blessing, you say it in the present tense and say what you want to become reality. What I want is for the person to live in integrity and compassion. Now I have no idea what effect that had on them, but I know that when I called my credit card company, they quickly reversed the charges and took care of the situation. I was able to let go of any anger I might have felt and instead send love. When we hold on to anger, it is like taking poison and expecting the other person to feel sick. It is like worry and fear; it doesn't help us when we hold on to it.

When you send blessings, it must be from the heart and full of love. When you have that feeling of worry in the pit of your stomach, change it into a blessing. Perhaps you are worried about your child who is traveling. Instead of dwelling on worry, send a blessing. Send a blessing that they see themselves as a perfect expression of Source, that they are surrounded by love, and that whatever is in their highest good is what will happen.

Blessings of gratitude are also powerful. Send blessings of gratitude for the day, your home, your relationships, the challenges that you are going through because of the wonderful lesson they reveal to you — anything for which you are grateful.

I send blessings as I'm driving. If you have someone cut you off in traffic, it is much more productive to send them a blessing that they see themselves as a perfect expression of Source and loved by the universe than to cuss them out and raise a certain finger in their direction. Most of the time, they will not even realize that you are angry, but they will feel the faint glow of the love you just sent them, and *you* will feel the love, too.

Try sending blessings when you think about someone or when you are in a place with lots of people. Many days, on my way to work, I sent a blessing that Bayaud is a place where all people are loved and valued, where all staff is in their right job, and it is a place of abundance well used. I have been sending blessings for over nine years now. It has made such a difference in my life. What I have noticed since I started doing this is that I am no longer competitive with my co-workers. I can truly celebrate the greatness in them without fear that it takes away anything from me. It has added so much more love in my life and there is always room for that!

Alex has taught me a great deal about letting go and how sending blessings can help. He also provides opportunities for me to practice this — like the time he had watched the *Stuart Little 2* movie about four times that day and at least that many times for the preceding five days. In the movie, Stuart Little meets a new friend who is a small bird named Margalo. She has been under the control of a falcon who is quite mean. Alex had been sitting, staring out our back door at the two girls jumping on the trampoline in the yard of the neighbor behind us. Up to this point, we had waved and said "Hi" over the fence to this neighbor, but that was all. We certainly would not have recognized each other at the grocery store; we didn't really know what each other looked like up close.

Alex decided he needed to go 'warn the girls,' probably about the falcon, but he didn't say. He just got up and proceeded to walk out the front door and around the block to their house. I let my husband know what was going on, made sure I had my cell phone, and followed Alex. He found the house and right before walking up to the front door, he told me he had to go to the bathroom. My first thought was, "Are you f@#ing kidding me!" It had taken us about 15 minutes to walk around the block to their house; there was no way he had time to walk home. So, he walked up to their front door and rang the doorbell. Did I mention it was also dinner time and we did know that they were in the middle of remodeling their kitchen and living room, so things were a little crazy?

The way I 'let go' was as Alex was walking up to the door, I sent blessings that this family lived in love and compassion, blessings that whatever was in Alex's highest good is what would happen and blessings that I would calm down.

The man of the house opened the door. I said, "Alex believes he needs to warn your daughters about something; he has been watching *Stuart Little 2* which means he probably wants to warn them about the falcon and he needs to go to the bathroom." Just what you expect to come out of the mouth of strangers who ring your doorbell? With a very puzzled look on his face, he graciously said Alex could come in and use the bathroom. By this time, his wife had come to the door, and I explained more about what was going on as the husband went back to the work of remodeling.

The wife was so kind; she told Alex he could go to the backyard where the girls were still on the trampoline. After he went to the bathroom, he quickly went to the trampoline and began jumping. The two girls were wonderful with him. They didn't judge him; they just accepted him and let him be. The wife then introduced me to her other children, a little baby girl and a 13-year-old boy who also had disabilities (he is developmentally delayed and has behavior issues). Suddenly it was clear why they were all so kind and accepting. They got it!

I could have really freaked out about this entire situation. This is certainly not in any books on proper etiquette. But it works when we let go of fear and be open to the mystery. Did Alex know that they would be accepting of him? Or is he just lucky? I don't know the answer to that, but the night did end with us exchanging phone numbers and planning a movie night for some time in the future.

There have been other times like this, when Alex does something that on the outside seems crazy, but when I just let it unfold as it will and send blessings, something good comes from it. I guess the lesson is that the more we can trust the universe to send us down paths that will serve us in some way, the more open we are to let go of our urge to freak out and instead step forward in faith and love.

While I was writing this book, I was trying to get the formatting correct. I was getting frustrated and pulling my hair out, visibly upset. Alex came up and stood beside me. He asked me what was wrong. I told him that the book I was working on about him and his sisters was frustrating me. He didn't say anything but grabbed a yellow sticky and a pen and wrote: Alex Katy Alle (he doesn't quite spell Alli's name right). He was reminding me to let go of all the little things that can get in our way and focus on what's important: Alex, Katy, and Alli. Thanks, Alex, for gently showing me the importance of letting go!

LIFE BITES:

- Let go of our need for perfection and worry.
- Remember that the universe always has our back and that things are always working out for us, even if that means walking through challenging times empowering each other.
- Send blessings, like "I love you and I send you blessings that you see yourself as the perfect expression of Spirit that only you are, that your voice is heard, and your talents are shared in ways that make the world a better place."
- Here is another blessing I use anytime I see a police officer or other emergency personnel, "I send you blessings that you are in your right job, that you live in integrity and compassion. Blessings of gratitude for how you keep our communities safe and blessings for safety in your job."

THE IMPORTANCE OF DISAPPOINTMENT AND FAILURE

There will be days when you are disappointed with yourself or your child or someone else for a variety of reasons. One of Alex's first therapists who came into our home was a woman named Mickie who herself had a child with Down syndrome. She taught us a phrase that had helped her tremendously with her own son. The phrase was *This too shall pass*. So true! Almost nothing lasts forever. Don't ignore the disappointment; feel it, learn from it, and let it go.

It is also important for our children to feel disappointment. This is a natural part of life. Let them feel it when they are young so they know they will survive it as they get older. Let them know they can move through it and it doesn't have to ruin their day. If they never feel disappointment in childhood, it will possibly be scary for *you* the first time they feel it as a teenager. It can trigger these lovely things called 'a behavior.' Believe me, 'a behavior' is not any of our goals. As a matter of fact, avoiding 'a behavior' is definitely preferable! But, again, life happens and if 'a behavior' happens you will survive, and this too shall pass! (See how handy that was!) 'Behaviors' are so important they have their own chapter; just wait a bit.

Allowing your child to experience disappointments also helps prepare them for work someday. The whole process of finding work and doing work has built-in disappointments. For instance, you don't get the job you know you'd be perfect for, or you can't just do your favorite part of your job and ignore the rest. I remember one time I was job coaching a young man with autism. (A job coach is someone who goes to work alongside someone with a disability to help him learn the job and determine what type of accommodations might be required).

I was coaching him on how to work at a chocolate factory. One of his tasks was to replace the box at the end of the conveyor belt so that it would catch the chocolates cascading into it. It was great fun (except for the time it started going too fast and we looked very much like Lucy and Ethel in that famous scene from the Lucy Show!) But the other job he had to do was feed plastic bubble wrap into this machine that recycled it. As you fed the plastic in, the pops it created were so loud it sounded like gun shots, which scared him. He said in a loud, dramatic voice, "I'm not in love with this machine!" It was disappointment at its finest, but still a part of the job that needed done.

Another woman I worked with collected shoe boxes. I took her to a shoe store to apply for a stocking job, no pun intended. While she was applying, she asked if there were any shoe boxes she could have. The manager looked around but found no boxes for her. She was so upset it was all I could do to keep her on task enough to complete the application. I am sure that the behavior she displayed kept her from getting the job. You could tell she was used to getting her own way and *NOT* used to disappointment!

When Alex was about 10, we tried to take him to an ice-skating show. He was so excited about going! But when we got to the venue, there was nothing there. I must have had the wrong date for the event. I was afraid he was not going to take it well, but he did fine. We talked about other things that we could do which worked to distract him. It was a small chance to practice how to live through disappointment and make the best of it.

One time, when Katy was a teenager, her school was planning to go on a big trip through the southwest. It was a school based on Outward Bounds principals called Rocky Mountain School of Expeditionary Learning, RMSEL, so they go on trips often. She was really looking forward to it, but then was unable to go because she was recovering from back surgery. I thought she would have a really bad attitude about it, but she didn't. She made the best of the situation and moved on. I believe that Katy going through all the medical challenges that she had been through at that point (allergic reactions and multiple surgeries) had taught her how to deal with disappointment in a healthy way.

In junior high, Alli went to our local public school. This was not a good fit for Alli. Disappointment was part of her daily life. She was disappointed that teachers didn't really know how to teach her or appreciate her unique abilities. I remember when my husband and I took her to a parent-teacher conference. The teacher said, "Has she always been this slow?" I couldn't believe she had said that right in front of Alli! Disappointment was part of daily life for Alli until she found RMSEL. It was a place where they celebrated her uniqueness. It was a place where book smarts weren't the only important trait; they also focused on service and character. After going through such disappointment, RMSEL was a huge gift to her!

To finally be appreciated and supported for who she truly was felt awesome. Alli excelled in high school, learning Spanish so quickly people thought we must speak it at home. As she learned how to deal with disappointment, she learned how courageous she was and that she has something of value to give the world.

Allow your children to feel disappointment. Help them to see that there is a gift in everything we go through. That will take them much farther than doing everything you can to make sure they never feel disappointment at all.

Failure is similar to disappointment. It is equally important to have them experience failure and see that it's not the end of the world. Failure happens at work and in life. It is a natural part of the learning process. If we have never failed in life, we have not tried very hard. I have failed many times in my life.

I have tried a number of different network marketing companies selling everything from nutritional supplements to mutual funds and life insurance. Theoretically, I have what it takes to succeed at these ventures. I know a lot of people, I will talk to anyone anywhere, and I love to learn new things. But the truth is I did fail and led my family into bankruptcy which was a challenging time for all of us. I felt guilty about this for a long time. But I learned things when we went through bankruptcy that nothing else could have taught me. I learned that I like to work for a company that gives me a paycheck on a regular basis, especially when it lets me do the things I do well, like facilitate classes and figure out what jobs are a good fit for a person. I have a deeper appreciation for companies and all that goes into creating a successful business because I now know more about how challenging it can be.

When our children participate in sports where everyone wins, what are we teaching them? It isn't about winning all the time, but it is about real life and in real life, people win and people lose. They are not going to 'win' every job they apply for or be able to date every girl or boyfriend they want. Sometimes losing teaches us that we want to try harder to win or that maybe we don't really want something. Think about all the jobs you have applied for or the girl/boyfriend you tried to pursue. Would you really have wanted them all? I'm not talking about creating super competitive people, but some healthy competition brings out the best in all of us even if we are just competing with ourselves. It is another chance for our children to learn that just because they didn't 'win' doesn't mean they didn't have fun or learn something. It teaches them more lessons about real life.

People with disabilities have usually failed at things. They may have failed at learning to walk or talk as quickly as their siblings or cousins. That is okay! That is how they learn — in their own time and in their own way. As they grow, make sure to give them room to fail in a space where it is safe and acceptable.

LIFE BITES:

- Disappointment is a natural part of life and learning.
- Allow your children to feel disappointment. Help them to see that there is a gift in everything we go through.
- Failure can be a great teacher. Help your children find the lesson in the failure.
- In real life, people win and people lose and that's a good thing.
- Let your children know they failed, but *they* are not a failure.

HELP AND SUPPORT

Raising three children with the challenges that our children have is not something my husband and I could have done alone. It would not have been possible! We had to have help and support. I had to take a dose of humility and let in people who were willing to be there for us. My husband and I had to lean into each other when we were having a difficult time dealing with something. There were times when he would really struggle with everything and times when I would. In those times, leaning on each other for strength and encouragement was critical. We also had to reach out to other people and agencies for support.

One of the most significant forms of support we have received is being paid to care for Alex which started when he was 14 years old. We first went through a program through Medicaid Long Term Care called the HCBS—EBD waiver which stands for Home and Community Based Services—Elderly, Blind, and Disabled waiver. There are other waivers for various conditions, like brain injury, depending on your state. This allowed Alex's sisters and me to get paid a few hours a week to care for Alex. This helped us so much financially. It was a total of about $1000 a month which was quite helpful. In this program, an outside agency hires family members or others to care for your child. They must have significant disabilities, including medical issues. You are not paid to just watch your child.

Then when Alex was 21, we learned about the CDASS program mentioned in the introduction. This program is different because the person with the disability or a family member is actually the employer. They are able to decide who will care for the person with a disability. Since there is no middle agency, like there is with the other program, more of the money goes to the care of the person, so they qualify for more paid hours. Alex received around 24 hours a week through the

HCBS—EBD program. Through the CDASS program, he qualified for 35 hours a week.

This is what has allowed Fred to get paid to stay home with him. I no longer have to try to get Alex out of the house to go to school or a day program which could take hours and possibly trigger a behavior which occasionally required the assistance of a police officer to calm Alex down. I can now go to work on time just about every day. There are still times when something is going on that makes it difficult for me to leave, but that is now a rare occurrence.

Sometimes our family requires help when we least expect it. When Alex was about 12 years old, he had 'a behavior' in a beautiful little town called Morrison at the foot of the mountains in Colorado. We were there to go on a hike and then to an ice cream shop. It was me, Alex, and his twin sister, Katy. He was hitting us and throwing rocks at us. We were scared and didn't know what to do. It was quite obvious to people passing by that we needed help. Not everyone who sees this will help. They are afraid and not sure what to do or don't want to get involved, you know — the thoughts that go through all of our heads when we see someone having an issue.

But there was a man and a woman who did stop and ask if we needed assistance. We knew that we needed to get Alex calmed down as much as possible and into our car. The problem was that our car was parked several blocks away. This wonderful woman that I shall never forget andyet not even know her name, offered to go and get the car for us. It allowed her, and the others who stopped to help, to be the heroes we needed at that moment. It allowed me to see how wonderful people can be when they are given the chance. I had to be open for help and the lesson it taught me was doing it alone was not an option. I also was able to let go of the shame that I felt for needing such help and not being able to control my child. I had to once again embrace being an imperfect parent and learn to love myself through it all.

You will need help; every one of us needs help at one time or another. Ask for it when you need it. Try to avoid asking in that manipulative, passive/aggressive way. Instead of saying, "I'm fine, I don't need any help," when you know that is not true, be direct and say what you need help with. Ask from a place of personal power, not from the victim stance. In other words, ask for help directly and from a place of love and gratitude, not from a place where you feel weak and want to 'guilt' the other person into helping you.

When the twins were about three years old and in preschool, they had to be transported from preschool to daycare at about noon each day. My husband and I both worked and there was no way we could make that happen and keep our jobs. I had to let go of the illusion that I could somehow do it all myself so I had to tell one of the other mothers from preschool about my dilemma. She offered to take both Katy and Alex to daycare every day. It meant the world to me, but if I had not asked, or if I had said, "I'm fine, I don't need help," I would have been screwed and probably lost my job.

One of the things that I have learned is that when you need help and ask for it, it allows some beautiful person to move through grace and make a difference in your life. You have allowed the natural flow of the universe to happen. You have received and another has given, allowing you both to remember that we are all connected and that giving feels good! To me, grace is that energy that allows you to go through the challenging moments of your life and learn from them to become more of who you are. When you allow another to help you, it allows that person to also move through grace and humbly be of service to another. As the saying goes, "It is better to give than to receive." But if no one ever needed help, we wouldn't have opportunities to experience this.

Another thing that is awesome is when someone offers help when you don't even ask! I remember this nice lady from church, Martha, who offered to take my children for the afternoon one Sunday after church when Alli was ten and the twins were three years old. It was around Christmas time before my mother had moved to Denver. I was so surprised and grateful I cried. It was such a great gift to have a few moments to myself. My mother, who moved to the Denver area when the twins were 4 and Alli was 11, is also wonderful at offering to help before we ask. Just a few minutes ago, my mom came and picked up Alex and took him to her house without being asked. It is wonderful! Now I can write in peace and quiet.

Before the twins were born, I believed I was a strong, independent woman who would not admit to needing help. I had lived my life with a desire, almost a desperation, to be strong, definitely judgmental of those around me who needed any type of assistance. What strength meant to me then was being strong enough, set in my ways enough, to not let others control me or even help me. But then life happened, the twins were born, and I woke up to reality. I gained some humility, let go of some judgment, and learned to accept help.

I am realizing that real strength is having the courage to be awake to who I authentically am, feeling what I am feeling in each moment — accepting the emotion, really feeling it and then releasing it so it doesn't get stuffed down into our bodies; knowing that there are moments of vulnerability where the strongest thing I can do is lean into those I love, allowing their strength to support me even if just for a moment; allowing myself the courage to not be the person that has to 'fix' everyone's problems. Indeed, none of us are here to 'fix' anyone else. I am here to be the best version of myself that I can be. I can allow the strength of others to lift me up. I can be open and know my own worthiness, even in the most vulnerable of moments, to allow in all the good the universe/God/Source has waiting for me.

Knowing I am worthy, being grateful, releasing any doubt and fear, opens the door to allow that help to flow in and me being able to accept it. My intention is to open that door with deep appreciation of all I truly am, knowing that real strength is found in connection with others. When we are judging someone, we can't be truly connecting with them or loving them. I would rather be love. What a great lesson to learn.

Where are some places you look for help and support? One of the places where we received support was a parent group called Pilot Parents which I mentioned before. It was a group of parents of kiddos with all types of disabilities. It was great to be around other parents who had important information about resources and how to deal with all the changes in our lives and everything else involved in raising kids. We figured things out together. This was crucial for Fred and me when our children were young and all of this was new to us. It helped us work through our feelings and find the hope and humor.

Life has changed a great deal for people with disabilities in the past 30 years even though we still have a long way to go. Alex was born by c-section in 1993. Because of the surgery, I was under anesthesia at the time of his birth. Fred told me that the doctors determined quickly that he probably had Down syndrome because of the extra skin on his neck and the shape of his ears.

Fred was wandering the halls of the hospital after the birth when an intern tracked him down and told him, "We need to talk. We believe your son has Down syndrome. We need to do some x-rays of his brain to make sure there's something up there." Then he kept talking and through a great deal of innuendo basically asked if we wanted to 'get rid' of Alex. Fred said, "No, we're good." He determined right then that he would have to get with the diagnosis or not. Fred chose in that moment to get with it! Can you imagine? I know that life can be a challenge with Alex, but I certainly can't imagine life without him!

We now have laws like the Americans with Disabilities Act (the ADA). Here is what the ada.gov website says about it:

> The Americans with Disabilities Act of 1990 (ADA) prohibits discrimination and ensures equal opportunity for persons with disabilities in employment, State and local government services, public accommodations, commercial facilities, and transportation.

Because of this law, we now have the support of our local school districts and other government agencies like the State Department of Vocational Rehabilitation which can help your child find work or training when they reach 18. They also have a youth program that starts at age 14.

We have the support of this law which says that public buildings and transportation need to be accessible. This law has been a great starting point in supporting those with disabilities to have a more integrated and higher quality of life. Even though we still have work to do, it is important to remember how far we have come!

LIFE BITES:

- It is ok to ask for help! It is not a sign of weakness but rather an opportunity for grace.
- Research the help that is available for your child through various agencies and programs. Ask other parents about resources they have used.
- Remember that real strength is admitting to our vulnerable moments and lean into those we love. I can allow the strength of others to lift me up.
- Knowing I am worthy, being grateful, releasing any doubt and fear, opens the door to allow good to flow to me. Being able to accept it is key
- My intention is to open that door with deep appreciation of all I truly am, knowing that real strength is found in connection with others.

DOCTORS AND OTHER PROFESSIONALS

Doctors and other professionals are important, helpful, life-changing individuals. They can give you the tools that you will need to not only survive this journey, but also help you and your child to thrive. Are they all that awesome? Nope, but some are, so focus on that.

Don't be afraid to ask questions, even question their suggestions—respectfully, of course. The ear, nose and throat doctor who told Alex he was obese wanted to take out his tonsils to possibly improve Alex's breathing. I asked him what Alex would eat during recovery since he eats nothing soft. He doesn't eat yogurt or ice cream or mashed potatoes and he is diabetic so not eating at all can be a problem. The doctor responded, "That is more complicated than I thought." And no surgery was done.

When you meet with a doctor, have a list of questions ready which you want answered. Doctors do not typically have ample time to spend with each patient, which can be a little intimidating. It is helpful to have questions ready; this keeps you on track to get them answered. It is also helpful to bring something quiet for your child to play with. Alex loves to tie and untie a colorful shoelace, which is great because it is quiet and something he can do alone. Other things that might work are soft things you can gently throw while you wait, like a little beanie baby or a soft, small ball, or a doll, or paper and markers to draw. This will help pass the time while you wait and hopefully allow you to focus on what the doctor is saying when they finally do begin the examination.

In my experience, it has been beneficial to be open to other types of healing that may help as well. Do your research though. There are great things out there, but there are also scams. Keep your mind and eyes open. Talk to people who have used the method of healing you are researching. What does the person have to gain from what they are telling you? Are they selling something? Not that there is anything wrong with making a buck but be more discerning. Look at reviews online for their product or services, which is a good way to get objective information. But take that with a grain of salt, too. One or two bad reviews doesn't necessarily mean the product/service is bad; it may just be a grumpy person giving the review.

Here are a few things that have been successful with our kids. These are not advertisements and I will not receive any financial compensation for mentioning them; they are just what has helped our family:

AIM: This is an energy healing program that uses the person's picture and various frequencies to allow the body to heal. About a month after Alex was on AIM, a Planters wart that was on his big toe disappeared and never returned. It also appears to have helped lower his A1c levels, which is a test to show average blood sugar levels over time. Our entire family has been on it for about nine years. We seem to stay healthier and have more of a sense of well-being. Here is the website: http://aimforjoy.com/

Emotion Code: This is a technique that you can use to remove emotional blocks from your body using muscle testing and a chart that shows various emotions. There are Youtube videos showing how to do this technique. I have used this with Katy, Alex, and myself. It helped Alex with letting go of some anger and sleeping better. It helped Katy with some pain relief and me with letting go of some long-held issues that I didn't even realize were an issue. I love this technique because you can do it at home, it doesn't cost money, and you can let go of emotions without having to relive the emotions and events that created them. Here is the website for Dr. Bradley Nelson who created the Emotion Code and has written a book about it: http://www.drbradleynelson.com/

Herbs and supplements: I can't imagine life without herbs and supplements! They have helped me and my children immensely. You need to make sure that what you are taking is bioavailable. Most vitamin and mineral pills that you buy at the store and take are *not* well absorbed by your body, so you end up just pooping them out. This can lead to expensive poop, not what you want! Taking things in powder or liquid form are usually better. Making sure that you take things together that need each other to be effective is also important. It is a good idea to seek the guidance of a professional to help determine what is needed. The websites that I have used that have good products at reasonable prices are Vitacost.com and Bulksupplements.com. I have also used a couple of network marketing companies in the past who do have great products, but they are expensive.

We have recently started using minerals from Mother Earth Minerals, meminerals.com. These are the best and most effective supplements we have ever used! They help with mood, sleep, energy, and more. They come in liquid form, so you put a dropper full under your tongue — no pills to swallow. Their website is helpful and they offer a book, *Wellness Secrets for Life*, by A. True Ott PhD., that explains the products and how to use them.

Acupuncture: When all three of our kids were young, they had the acupuncture treatments to alleviate allergies, which was helpful. Katy has done acupuncture for her back and other issues and Fred did acupuncture to release toxins. Make sure to find a reputable acupuncturist.

EFT Tapping: According to thetappingsolution.com website, Emotional Freedom Technique (EFT) Tapping is a powerful holistic healing technique that has been proven to effectively resolve a range of issues, including stress, anxiety, phobias, emotional disorders, chronic pain, addiction, weight control, and limiting beliefs. It is based on the combined principles of ancient Chinese acupressure and modern psychology. You tap on specific meridian endpoints of the body using your fingertips while focusing on negative emotions or physical sensations to help calm the nervous system and rewire the brain to respond in healthier ways.

Tapping has helped me personally with addiction to sweets, pain alleviation, getting to sleep, etc. The tapping technique I used to stop emotional eating is from Brittany Watkins. You can find it on Youtube; search Brittany Watkins Emotional Eating. I did this technique one time and I no longer feel like I have to have sweets. I can even pass on cake when it is someone's birthday at work — something I had never done before! It definitely feels good to have a healthier relationship to sweets.

There are some great things about tapping. Once you know what you are doing, you can do it for free anytime, anywhere! You can also do surrogate tapping, where you tap for the benefit of another person. I know it sounds weird, but intention is a powerful thing. Try it; you really have nothing to lose.

Along with healing professionals, there are also professionals who help your child in the school setting. You will meet with them at least annually. You will all convene at the annual Individualized Education Program (IEP) meeting. This meeting determines how your child will spend their days at school so it is important. These meetings include some or all of the following professionals:

- The parents are an important part of this meeting and the IEP. We help determine appropriate goals for our child and then see if they are accomplished.
- Speech pathologists help the child with pronunciation and articulation so that the child's speech can be understood or if speech is not possible, they determine alternative technology so that the child can express themselves (there are various types of assistive technologies for this).
- The occupational therapist's job is to determine how to help the child do things they need to do, like how to eat with a spoon or write with a pencil, etc. It may mean finding a curved spoon so that the child can more easily get food into their mouths or use a pencil with a plastic ring on it to make it easier to hold. They are creative problem solvers.
- Physical therapists are focused on how to help your child move in more efficient ways. They work with your child on walking or reaching — all things related to physical movement. They, too, are creative problem solvers.
- School psychologists perform the IQ tests and other psychological tests on your child to determine eligibility and the appropriate services for the child. They may also counsel the child throughout the school year if that is necessary. They may be observing how the child is reacting at the meeting as well.
- Learning specialists may be necessary if your child has learning challenges; they provide strategies that will be most effective in helping your child to learn.

- Social workers will take note of family history — how the child interacts with other children and adults. They will be more involved if the child has behavioral issues or if the family requires additional resources.
- The regular ed teacher is the teacher whose classroom your child is in some of the time along with children who are not in Special Ed. The amount of time depends on the needs of the child and sometimes, the needs of the school.
- The Special Ed teacher has more training in how to deal with the needs of your child. Your child will probably spend some percentage of their day in the Special Ed classroom.
- There may be others involved, like an audiologist if the child has hearing issues, mobility specialist if they use assistance (like a wheelchair or walker) to get around, a school nurse if there are health issues like diabetes, etc.

(Some of this information is from the verywell.com website where they have a section on Meet Your IEP Team which has helpful information.)

The Special and Regular Ed teachers, possibly speech, occupational and physical therapists will see your child weekly, if not daily, and know them well. Some of the professionals included just come in occasionally to evaluate how things are going, like the psychologist, learning specialist and social worker. They are still an important piece to make sure the IEP is being followed.

These professionals sit around, telling you all about your child's strengths and weaknesses with suggestions of what you should or should not be doing. I have been to many of these for my children and although it may come as a shock, they are really not meant to make you cry! They just sometimes seem that way. Try not to take them personally, learn from them, and acknowledge what you are doing well already. Your child has a challenge; that's why the meeting is necessary. Everyone sitting at the table knows raising our children isn't easy which is why they are there. You can even ask for an advocate to be with you if you feel that would be helpful. In our community, the Arc has advocates who will join you in these meetings.

If you believe they should know something about your situation, perhaps you have a disability yourself or you have other children with challenges, tell them. They may be able to help you figure out how to balance it all or get you extra help. Remember if you don't ask, it's not going to happen. These meetings can bring up many different emotions. It's always important to talk about what you're feeling to an appropriate person — maybe another parent, your spouse, friend, or therapist. My mother has been an incredible support for me. She understands but also doesn't just let me have a long pity party. She helps me work through my feelings, reframe the situation, and move on. Not everyone has someone in their family who can listen to their feelings without judgment and be helpful, but reach out to someone who will listen — perhaps another parent or friend.

Reframing the situation is when you change the way you look at what is going on and find positive aspects or lessons that you can learn from it. For example, at one IEP, they told us to make labels for many items around the house, like *door, drawer, light*, etc. This felt overwhelming to me considering I had two five-year-olds at home, a 12-year-old who needed help with homework, and I worked a full-time job! When I thought about how to reframe it, I thought about making it a fun project for all of us to do. My oldest daughter could help figure out what things we would label, I would write them on paper, and the twins could help tape them where they belong. It was still a big task, but we reframed it to be a more positive, fun experience.

Professionals like physical, occupational and speech therapists, teachers, and others, can have wonderful suggestions, but sometimes they are difficult to carry out. Do what you can, what makes the most sense, and let go of the guilt! I really doubt that you will ever receive a Mother's or Father's Day card from your child that says, "Gosh, you are the best mom/dad ever! If only you had followed all the speech therapist's instructions so I could properly say my R's!"

The trick is to not beat yourself up but be patient with yourself and your child. There were many times when I left an IEP meeting feeling like the worst parent on the planet. I would cry all the way home! But parenting is not something any of us will do perfectly all the time. We will all have moments of brilliance followed by moments of doubt.

Reframe the situation and make the best out of it to the best of your ability unless you are just too tired. If that's the case, just try to take a nap! This too shall pass! (See how handy that can be!)

Speech therapists say to label things in your house; physical therapists tell us to move our kid's legs this way or that as they lie on the floor; all kinds of other well-meaning professionals want us to do something that at the moment seems important. But they may not realize we have other children to deal with or jobs we must go to and so their priorities do not become ours and we don't do what we've been instructed to do. We feel inadequate. I believe that looking back over the first few years of Alex's life, I see that the most important thing we can do is love our child, all our children, completely and unconditionally. Take time to love our spouses who can sometimes get lost in the shuffle of all this, because another great gift we can give all our children is a healthy and loving relationship between their parents. And if it's not healthy for the relationship to stay intact, part as gracefully as possible, without having life become a battleground.

Therapies will come and go; do what you can and what makes sense, but what your children will remember most is the love they felt. That is what gives all of us the strength to be our best selves.

LIFE BITES:

- Ask professionals you deal with questions, respectfully of course, and have a list of questions ready. If you don't ask, it's not going to happen.
- Be open to other types of healing modalities, but question them, especially if they sound too good to be true.
- We will all have moments of brilliance followed by moments of doubt. Do what you can and what makes sense and let go of the guilt!
- The most important thing is to love your child unconditionally.

FOOD'S NEW MEANING

To a person with disabilities, food can be:

- A challenge
- A control issue
- Tied to their emotions, (and ours)
- Difficult because of sensory issues
- Affected greatly by medicines
- A life-or-death situation because of allergies
- A source of joy

What can you do about it?

From as early as you can, offer a variety of foods, but *don't* force your child to eat it. That can create a control issue which can be quite challenging and can last a lifetime. As the old saying goes, "You can lead a horse to water, but you can't make him drink!" Instead, help your children have control over what they eat, within reason. For instance, give them a choice between peas or broccoli with their favorite macaroni and cheese. Get them involved in what the family eats. Ask if they want to help plan a menu for dinner, talk about the various food choices, and why having different foods is good for their body. On a piece of paper, you can write:

Protein _____

Carbs _____

Vegetables or Fruit _____

Then together, help fill in the blanks. This will help them learn about healthy eating and having control over what they eat; both skills will help them in life. There is a video on YouTube called Healthy Eating for Kids, by Smile and Learn. You could watch this together to learn more about healthy eating, and then work on your menu.

If your child is able, it may encourage them to eat if they have helped you prepare the meal. This may just mean opening a package, stirring something, or adding some ingredient to the mix. Having your child help in some way also is good to prepare them for employment someday. Make sure, if they are helping cook, that you instill safe cooking habits like washing hands before cooking, washing surfaces before and after using them, and taking extra care to clean after raw meat has been in contact with a surface. If they are actually cooking, tell them to make sure to turn off burners, stove, etc., when they are finished and to always have a cooking buddy with them.

Encourage your child to try new things but try to keep it from being a control issue. Offer new things by having them available and praising them if they try them. Sometimes it works to just put the new thing in front of them and not say anything about it. You can also encourage them to try just one bite and let you know what they think of it. Even getting them to eat one bite is a victory and keeps the door open for them to continue to try new things.

I know a woman who was raised on a macrobiotic diet. According to Webmd.com, this is a diet based on whole grains, vegetables, and beans as well as maintaining a positive attitude and a balanced life. From a child's perspective, this is a diet based on no birthday cakes, or pudding or dessert, *ever*. This was not the child's desire, so the child did it while she was home, but once she got out on her own, she ate everything she had been kept from her whole life. She is now obese and continues to struggle with having a healthy relationship to food and maintaining a healthy weight. Would it have been better to offer her that type of diet and give her control over what part of it she accepted and then allowed her to have other types of food as well?

Alli dealt with bulimia for a few years. It began when she lost weight and people began giving her lots of attention regarding the weight loss. I had also said to her in the past that she should lose weight (something

I really regret saying). I'm sure that comment fed into the thought that she would be more loved if she could just lose more weight. Well, she got to a point where she could no longer lose weight in a healthy way and turned to bulimia. (This is when after eating you throw up your food.) I didn't realize this was going on until she finally told me, which was about three years after she began. I felt terrible that I hadn't been able to see her suffering like this! Alli had lost a great deal of weight, which I complimented her on. I didn't realize when I said that how she was doing it. When she told me, it was a shock! I couldn't believe that I had fed into the continuation of her feeling the need to do that!

Now I strive to not comment on anyone's weight, but instead focus on things that are more important and let them know that I love them right now as they are. Try instead to comment on someone's energy or intelligence or how kind they are or how you enjoy being around them or how great they are at solving problems. Things that, in the end, are far more important than the number on a scale. Alli stopped being bulimic on her own by learning to love herself. I make sure to let her know that I love her because she is so worthy of love.

If the lack of variety in your child's diet is because of sensory issues, or stubbornness, or something else, don't beat yourself up or worry too much. There may be supplements or vitamins that you can sneak into your child's food (like opening up capsules and putting the contents into their ketchup, yogurt or juice — just make sure that this won't affect the contents of the capsule or cause them to choke). We have also cut up pills and put them in Alex's chicken nuggets, although he sometimes complains about his chunky chicken nuggets. Be careful with this that the pills are small enough to not hurt their teeth if they bite into them. Alex doesn't chew very much, which is why this works for us.

There are now great websites and books to help you determine herbs, vitamins, and supplements that might be helpful to your child. Alex takes supplements that help with mood, diabetes, and sleep. They have helped him be happier, healthier, and have better blood sugar levels.

Don't forget the effect of the medicines our children take. In December 2015, when I took Alex to the psychiatrist, I told her I wanted to take him off the mood stabilizer he took every day and the antipsychotic medicine he took on an as-needed basis because it seemed to be making him gain weight. He was a little over 300 pounds at that point and had been on the medicine for six or seven years. The psychiatrist said, "Oh yes, those meds are a recipe for weight gain!" Really? Couldn't they have told me that 100 pounds ago? And why hadn't I brought it up 100 pounds ago? She replaced it with a medicine that is a mood stabilizer, but it also reduces his appetite. He has now lost 20 pounds in four months with no other changes. If your child's appetite or weight has changed, make sure to ask the doctor if it could be due to the medicines that they take.

Alex loves chicken nuggets, but he occasionally will try other foods. He also loves his burgers and fries, which is not likely to change. Even though I know he would be healthier if he never had those again, it is not realistic to get him to stop. His chicken nuggets, burgers, and fries are a source of joy for him, which is another reason to let him keep eating them. Deal with what you have. Offer healthy foods to go along with the foods they love and won't give up. You can also give supplements to make sure they are getting more of what their bodies need.

There are many people these days with food sensitivities or allergies. Both of my daughters are sensitive to gluten which means that when they eat gluten(basically things containing flour), they would get stomach aches, headaches, joint pain, and other symptoms. These days, it is a fairly easy ingredient to avoid because there are many wonderful substitutes (even bread continues to get better!). If you think it might be an issue for your child, have them not eat it for four to seven days and see if they feel better. A doctor will do a blood test for celiac disease which is a condition where any amount of gluten will make the person very sick. A celiac test will not show if the person is just sensitive to gluten. That is why avoiding gluten to see if they feel better may be well worth trying. Both of my daughters felt much better when they stopped eating gluten.

There are also food allergies that can be life threatening. Katy is allergic to almost any type of fish. One time, when she was a sophomore in high school, she was visiting a college campus . She shared food with one of her friends who had ordered both shrimp and chicken. She ate a piece of the chicken; up to this point she didn't know how allergic she was to shrimp. Even though she didn't eat the shrimp directly, there was cross contamination with the chicken. This led to an extremely severe allergic reaction that they had a hard time controlling. Finally, after three EpiPens and steroids, she was able to breathe. This was her first major reaction.

I have learned that there is no benefit to living our lives in fear and worry. They are truly wasted emotions if we hold onto them. They are useful if, when we feel worry or fear, we use those emotions to nudge us back onto the path of our lives, inspiring us to do what we know we need to do to get us where we have said we want to go. They are not useful when they paralyze us and keep us from moving forward.

One of the ways to release worry is to send a blessing, which we talked about in the chapter on Letting Go. In the case of food, you might send a blessing like this, "I send blessings to my child, that they see themselves as the perfect expression of Source, completely loved by the Universe. I send blessings that they will choose foods that will feed their body, mind, and soul. I release my need to control everything they eat, knowing that I will be guided to give them what is in their highest good." Feel free to change this to what feels right to your situation. In a perfect world, our kids would get the nutrition they need from the foods they eat, but my son has lived off of a diet of 70-80% chicken nuggets with two glasses of Naked Juice with some other supplements in it for over 10 years. He is healthy and even though he is a type 1 diabetic, his last A1c was 6.1 (which isn't bad!).

Some tips for helping your child have a healthy relationship to food:

- Model positive food choices (fast food is ok occasionally, but not more than once or twice a week if possible).
- Allow your child to have some control over what they eat.
- Listen to them when they say they don't like something. I made Katy eat crab when she was little, even though she said she really didn't want to. Not good! She said her throat hurt, even though there was no severe allergic reaction; she was definitely allergic to it.
- It is a beautiful idea to have everyone sit at the dinner table to eat together. Lots of studies have shown the value of this. Can I get my family to do it everyday? Not a chance. We're lucky to do it

on holidays and special occasions. I hope you have more luck in that department than I do!
- Remember moderation is a wonderful thing! It's okay to have soda pop or candy once in a while. It's okay to have burgers and fries once in a while. But it's not good to have them every day. Do what you can.

Hopefully, eating will be a pleasant experience in your home, at least some of the time!

LIFE BITES:

- Don't make food a control issue for you; allow your child some control over what they eat.
- Encourage your child to try new things and model good food choices.
- Don't put too much attention on weight loss but celebrate other great qualities in the person.

BECOME YOUR CHILD'S ADVOCATE

Being our children's advocate is such an important part of our job as parents. To me, advocacy is working with others to make sure all people are given a fair chance in education, health, and life in general. In other words, it is working with other people to make sure our children are treated like everyone else as much as possible. I say as much as possible because there can be issues with our kids that may make some things impossible.

For instance, with Alex, he was in a Special Ed classroom for about half the day when he was in high school; the rest of the time he was integrated into regular classrooms. This sounds great on paper and this is what advocates who had come before had fought for in our school systems. But for Alex, it was just too much. He was overwhelmed by all the people, especially the pretty girls, and the size of the large high school. Since he couldn't verbalize all this, he acted out instead and had serious behaviors. The first week of school, his freshman year, he pushed the vice principal down to the ground and threatened to hit her with a rock; thank goodness, he decided to drop the rock instead.

Because of this and other incidents, the district found a different school for him called Plum Creek Academy which is for young people with either emotional issues or dual diagnosis (meaning they have mental health diagnosis along with another type of disability). In Alex's case, he was there because he was developmentally delayed and had anxiety/mood disorder.

I am so glad the district placed him at Plum Creek. The staff there was amazing! It was a much smaller school; there were only six young people in Alex's class and about thirty on the side for students who require extra support for various reasons. The ratio of staff to students was much smaller than at the regular school. Alex still had some behavior issues but nothing as severe as the time with the vice principal.

Alex had advocated for himself in a way that made sure he was heard! He needed something different to survive and he got it. I don't know if there would have been a way for me to advocate for him to go to Plum Creek before he proved he needed it. And to tell the truth, I was afraid for Alex to go to such a school. I didn't know what it would be like for him, or for us, if he went there. What would the other students be like? Would there be a lot of violence? I am grateful I didn't let my fear stop him from going there because it was definitely the best place for him to be.

One of the things I have learned about advocating is to focus on the fact that everyone involved is trying to do what they believe is best for the children. This can foster developing effective solutions together instead of creating an "us and them" mentality where only one side can benefit. I have seen meetings where parents come in with the attitude that they are the only ones who really care for their child and everyone else has their own selfish agendas. But this is seldom the case because most people you will meet are doing the best they can with the information and tools they have. If you approach it with the attitude that we are all doing the best we can with the information we have, it is much easier for both sides to hear what the other is saying. Listening is more effective when you believe that everyone has the needs of the child in mind and deserves to be heard. Listening to each other is critical if you want to come up with workable solutions. You may not get 100% of what you want for your child, but you will get some of what you want and the solution will be more in line with the needs of the community.

One time, I was working with a young man who was employed at a fast-food restaurant. His mother was upset that once a day he would be required to go into the bathrooms and clean them if they needed it. She did not think that was proper work for a man to do, so she was advocating to the boss that he would not have to do it. The problem was she didn't know the truth of the situation. Every single employee who worked there, *including* the boss, was required to go into the restrooms daily to keep them clean. She was advocating for her son, but if she had listened to everyone, she would have realized that what she was advocating for was not fair to everyone else. Her son didn't mind doing the work; it was her idea that it was work that was beneath him, not his.

When you advocate for someone or a cause or a group of people, make sure you are really listening to what *they* want. Many years ago, I had the pleasure of meeting Craig Kielburger, who at the age of 12, began a non-profit organization called Free the Children which advocates for the rights of children.

He had read a newspaper article about a boy his age in Pakistan, Iqbal Masih, who had been shot and killed while riding his bike. Iqbal had been killed because he had spoken out against child labor. Craig really wanted to do something about it but he didn't want to assume he knew what the children wanted. He convinced his parents to allow him and an adult Canadian human rights worker, Alam Rahman, to go on a trip to Asia to meet the children who were working and hear from *them* what they wanted and needed.

He is a true advocate because he listened to what the children really needed and then advocated for them. His organization has built more than 300 schools, freed many children from child labor situations, and taught children all over the world that they have the power to make a difference. I encourage you to read his book *Free the Children,* or *Me to We*, or any of his other books. They are a great example of what each of us can do to make the world better and to advocate in ways that have the most positive impact on our communities.

Advocacy is critical and there are times when it may take a fight. One of those times is when it concerns the health of your child. When your child is sick, and you are fighting to get them the care they need, you can start out by listening and working to find solutions that are good for the community, but when it comes down to it, your child is worth a fight. We need to pick our battles as parents, with our children, families, professionals, etc. But, I believe, the battle for our child's health is the most important.

Katy went through a difficult time when she was dealing with severe allergies and pain issues. We would take her to all kinds of doctors, many of whom did not listen or believe her. The doctors did not believe she could have an allergic reaction from airborne smells of fish or marijuana. But she *did* have allergic reactions to these smells.

One time, Katy had been in a great deal of abdominal pain for several months. We would take her to the emergency room; they would look at her, possibly run a test or two and then send her home. They did tell us that abdominal pain is often undiagnosed. Finally, we went to an emergency room where the doctor said that it seemed like she was having gall bladder issues. He finally agreed to do the surgery and take it out. She had gall stones! They hadn't shown up on tests but she had them. Another doctor finally agreed to do surgery to help her endometriosis even though it had not shown up on tests either. The surgery helped alleviate a great deal of her pain. What the doctor also found was that it looked like she had had appendicitis that had healed so he also removed her appendix. That must have been a different time when we were in the emergency room and they sent her home.

Don't be afraid to talk to more than one doctor. Get a second opinion, research things on your own, and keep pursuing it until you get an answer or someone that at least listens! In our medical system, it seems like doctors are so specialized that they can only think about whatever they specialize in and have a hard time putting things together when more than one organ or biological system is involved.

I am a firm believer in other healing modalities like acupuncture, herbs, energy work, etc. I would love to see all types of healers working together on a person to determine the best course of action for their illness, including various types of healing modalities. For our kids who may have many things going on at the same time, it sure seems like it would create healthier outcomes.

LIFE BITES:

- Make sure to listen first and be open to what you hear.
- Believe all parties are doing the best that they can with the information they have available and determine solutions that move us all forward.
- Reach out to professional advocates to help you if needed.

- If it is for the health of your child or other important issues, do all that you can to gather information and keep going until you find a health professional or other professionals who will really listen to your concerns and take them seriously.

DISCIPLINE AND EMPLOYMENT

Setting boundaries, teaching your child self-discipline, and allowing them to experience failure and disappointment are critical if you want your child to be employable at some point in their life. These skills help to prepare them for the environment of work where everything doesn't always go your way; you must do some things you really don't want to do for a boss who isn't always nice. It is important to let your children know that *they* are not a disappointment or failure; they have experienced the emotions of disappointment and failure. They are not their emotions. This distinction can also help them feel the emotions of disappointment and failure without identifying themselves as disappointments or failures. This is a much healthier approach.

Teaching your child about boundaries is important so they understand things like setting boundaries around their own behaviors, and around relationships of all kinds, which allows them to function in society and at work. Boundaries and self-discipline are interconnected. You can't have one without the other. Showing your children ways to push through disappointment helps them find the blessing of work. To be needed, productive, hopefully appreciated, and earn a paycheck feels good to all of us. Work is an important part of most people's lives.

For the past twenty years, my job title has been job developer. I have helped over a thousand people, with all types of disabilities and those experiencing homelessness, find jobs. I also facilitate classes that provide many of the tools we all need to be successful in our jobs, like personal power, setting boundaries, and decision-making skills.

I was inspired to do this type of work by a keynote speaker I heard at a conference in 1994 for people on community-centered boards (CCB's). These are boards that control the money in a community that is designated for people who are developmentally delayed. This man, I don't recall his name, spoke about growing up in an institution because he was quadriplegic. He was incredibly intelligent and articulate, but he was not able to use his hands or legs and relied on a wheelchair and assistance to do many things most of us take for granted. He said that growing up he would not even allow himself to *dream* of having a job.

That really hit me! I had complained about my work so many times. At the time, I was a stockbroker at a discount brokerage firm. I had taken my job and my ability to work for granted. I knew then I wanted to do what I could to help open doors to employment for those with disabilities. It would take me about seven years before I had the courage to leave my comfortable job and find someone who would give me a chance to become a job developer.

I have learned over the years the beneficial qualities called soft skills that employers look for in employees. Here are some things we can do as parents to develop those qualities and create more easily-employable adults. These are also the skills that lead to a better quality, more empowered life.

Here is a list of ideas to help develop attributes important to employability:

- Allow your children to do what they are able to do on their own, like cut their own meat, do their laundry, and vacuum. They need to practice these activities to truly learn and get good at them. These are skills we, as adults, can do without thinking, but our children need more time to learn at that level. Give them the time they need. You may not be able to do this every time but do it as often as you can. These tasks won't be done as well as you do it at first, maybe ever, but it gives them a sense of responsibility and confidence in themselves. It also helps them develop their self-discipline.
- Teach them to listen and allow them to be heard. What ideas do they have? Alex is great at arranging furniture; we allow him to do that or at least add his input when we are rearranging furniture. This also models that it is important to listen to others.
- Give them room to explore their strengths. What are they naturally good at that they enjoy doing? What can you do to

help them develop those skills? For instance, if they are good at drawing, can they take a class at the local rec center? Can they use that skill in a way that gives them more responsibility — like maybe drawing greeting cards that they can send to relatives, or people in the service or a local assisted living facility? This would be a way to not only develop their skills, but also use them in a way that benefits others (which is what work is all about). Alex created a picture that we turned into a postcard that said, "We are all in this together. Let's let love lead," which we sent to over 700 people. We sent it to friends, relatives, people in nursing homes and assisted living facilities, and to people in prison. He got some amazing letters and phone calls back. It was a great experience and allowed him to see that he can make a difference.

- Allow them to try even if you think it's too much for them. I've worked with a number of people who are blind. If they had parents who allowed them to try things, even if it meant falling down and getting hurt, they are more successful and confident as adults. This is not an easy thing for us parents to do! You will read more about this in the Big Reveal chapter. This is a great lesson in boundaries. It allows them to set their own boundaries as far as what they feel is safe for them to do, boundaries of what others will do for them, and what they need to learn to do themselves.

- If you give your child an allowance with expectations attached, it helps teach responsibility and that it can be fun to work and earn money. If you sit down with your child to get their input about the chores for which they will be responsible, you may have more buy-in with them. For instance, if they say they want to help cook, you can add another related task like emptying the dishwasher. Then allow them to do it even if it is not perfect. Remind them to listen as you show them how to perform the chore so they can do it to the best of their ability and do it safely. If they help cook, make sure to teach them to wash their hands before and after handling food, to be safe around hot surfaces, and how to safely use knives if you think that is something they can do, and other kitchen safety tips. If you feel the need to go back and correct the work your child has done, be sly about it. Do it when they aren't home or are asleep. It isn't very motivating to have someone redo your work.

- To develop self-discipline, it is necessary to give our children choices. They need to be appropriate choices which might include what food they are going to eat, clothes to wear and working with them on when they need to turn off their electronic devices and talking about why that is important. When Alex was from about 10 years to 18 years old, I would hold out both of my hands in front of me with each one representing a choice he had. Then I would touch the first hand and use my fingers to walk up my arm as I said the first choice (which was the one I really wanted him to take, but you must be ready for him to choose the not-so-good choice). As my fingers walked up my arm I would say, "You can get your shoes on and get on the bus and then get the surprise that is waiting for you on the bus or," as I touched my other hand, "you can wait to get your shoes on until the bus leaves, I will then take you to school, but you won't get the surprise waiting for you." Then I would ask him to touch the hand that represented his choice. It is important that he knows either way, he is going to end up at school (which is what he was hoping to avoid). Then it is super important to follow through and do it even if it means he takes two hours to get his shoes on and get in the car! This is when it comes in handy to be a stay-at-home parent or work for a flexible boss (which is what I had). This is another lesson in boundaries. No matter what he did, he had to go to school; the boundary was set.

- Don't let them take things that don't belong to them. This sounds like common sense, but it is surprising how many people think because they work somewhere, they get to take whatever they want. This is a career limiting move for *any* of us! This includes drinking pop without permission if you work for a restaurant, taking pens and paper clips from an office, or eating someone else's lunch from the fridge. This can be a challenging thing to teach and a valuable lesson in boundaries! I know when Alex visits my brother's house, he always wants to take home one of their videos. This is a great time to tell him "no" and practice not getting what he wants. Sometimes, I would ask if it was okay for him to take a video; it is important that he understands that you *must* ask first. Sometimes I would tell him no, that he can watch the movie next time we visit. When you are at the doctor's office, don't let your child take a magazine. Remind them that it is there for everyone. It is great practice in living in integrity, a quality employers *love*.

A friend of mine, Becky Miller, who worked for a local community center board, told me about a client who was developmentally delayed; we'll call him Bob. He had a job coach which is the person who assists people with disabilities learn their job and help figure out accommodations and supports that might be necessary. Bob didn't get along with his job coach; we'll call him Ray. In this situation, the tendency is to change the job coach because as professionals, we think we are helping the individual when we take care of the problem ourselves, but that isn't what happened. The employer encouraged Bob to figure out a way to listen to Ray and work together. Bob was able to do that. The result was that Bob's self-esteem improved because someone believed he could resolve a problem and he learned about advocating for himself. It was okay for him to say, "This isn't working." And it was also okay to figure out a way to make it work.

When you are working with your child to guide them to find a job, allow them to own their own outcome, whether it is success or failure. Engage with them and respect their contribution. This shows them that they have value and worth. We don't have to do everything for them. Allowing our children to resolve their own issues is great for self-esteem as well as developing problem-solving skills.

For many people with ADD, ADHD, or dyslexia, they need to have variety in their job. They are often smart and great at solving problems. It may take them a little longer to learn things, but once it's learned, it stays with them. Finding jobs that are in line with their strengths and have variety is good. It is often important for them to work in an environment that gives them space and values their contribution.

One of the things that has helped Alli be successful in her job as a patient services lead for an ambulance company is to listen to music. This can be through headphones if allowed, or at a low volume so it doesn't bother co-workers but that she can hear. If that isn't possible, she sings songs in her head to entertain herself. She has found other unique ways to entertain herself, like putting sticky notes on her forehead, drawing on herself, using a squeeze ball or a fidget spinner. These things to others may look a bit strange but they help her concentrate and stay engaged which helps her do well in the job and remain doing the same work for many years. She also enjoys having a job with variety, which her current job does. The fact that she has ADD helps her do her job more effectively because she can focus on more than one thing at a time, like carrying on a conversation while entering data into the computer. When we give people with challenges a chance to work, they often bring unique perspectives and different valuable skills to the team.

Katy works as a skill development specialist with grade school children going through difficult situations. This might be having a parent with a drug addiction or illness or students who have other challenges themselves, like ADD or autism. She is able to bring her service dog, Justice, to work with her. His job is to smell allergens and warn Katy about them. The children love having Justice around! She then uses her own experience with challenges she had at school and all she learned from having a twin with Down syndrome to understand more of the supports her students need to be as successful as they can be. The things that she faced daily growing up in our house actually make her better at doing her job effectively.

It is important for you to consider *your* employment choices. It would be hard in many of our situations to have both parents working jobs where you have to be on time every day and not be able to leave work and come back occasionally. If you do both work jobs where there is no flexibility, you need to find support to help you, like possibly a retired grandparent or friend. For most of us with kids with challenges, this type of flexibility or assistance from others is critical to our own personal employment success.

When our kids were younger, I worked in the brokerage industry and Fred was a printer. This type of flexibility was impossible during our work hours but Fred worked nights for eleven years and for a few years I worked part time which allowed us the flexibility we needed. When Katy and Alex were in high school, and Alli had moved out of the house, Katy had monthly allergic reactions and several surgeries that required me to be with her during those times.

Alex would often take an hour or more to leave the house and get on the bus, if it was still there, to go to school. Sometimes the transition from leaving home to go to school led to full blown, violent behavior that required police intervention to de-escalate. During this time, I worked for Bayaud Enterprises which was a non-profit agency that works with people with disabilities, so they understood the challenges I was facing and gave me the flexibility my family required. I have had two wonderful, understanding bosses there which also helped me to keep my job. Because of these challenges though, I took my job seriously and did my best work to show my appreciation and not take my employment for granted. Those were very challenging times. Sometimes I am not sure how I got through them. But I did get through them and grew to be stronger, more empathetic, and not as afraid of things.

The fact that I have children with disabilities actually makes me better at my job because it gave me a deeper understanding of how to interact appropriately with people with disabilities. People with challenges want to be respected for their knowledge and abilities. Assume people know things; it is much more respectful than to assume they are not smart. I have more knowledge of accommodations that may be required and a greater openness to people's capabilities. The skills we learn from parenting our children are a benefit in many jobs, as well as the fact that we have learned a great deal about what is important in life and not to take as much for granted, which translates well at work.

A child who is developmentally delayed couldn't care less whether you are president of the United States, a dishwasher at Denney's, or unemployed, or writing a book on parenting kids with disabilities. They care if you spend time with them and that it is quality time. This can be a challenge for me and it has been more of a challenge as my children have grown up. When they were young, I expected to be home with them, but as they became adults, I thought they wouldn't need me home as much. With Alex, that isn't what happened. He still wants me home more than I am and paying more attention to him than I can and still accomplish the things I want to do. This is a balancing act, as is most of life.

One way I spend time with him is to sit on the couch beside him and read, write, or watch Youtube videos while he watches his iPad or video. This is not exactly quality time, but at least it is time with him. I also try to do something fun with him about once a week, like take him swimming or out to lunch. I try to do this with my daughters, mother, and husband once a month, too. Taking time to spend quality time with our loved ones is a worthy goal. It's okay if our book or other goal isn't finished today; it will get done, but we never know how much time we have with those we love.

One way to spend quality time with your children and develop skills that will help them be employable is to take your children places when they are young and expect them to get ready on time and get out to the car or bus. This will help *some* when they are older because they will have more experience with appropriate expectations, whether that is expecting them to use manners as they eat out, sit, and watch a movie or stay close to you at the zoo. Your expectations also need to be realistic based on their abilities — another great balancing act.

Teenage years are a tough time as far as getting them to do something they really don't want to do. Teenagers generally want to control their world as much as possible. That is natural, so make sure they have things they *can* control in their world. There are parents who try to control everything their child does until they move out for college or other reasons. What generally happens in those cases is that when the child is free to choose on their own, they haven't had experience with it and often do not make great choices. Giving children practice making choices throughout their life, helps them to know how to choose more wisely, at least more often. It also helps them learn to set boundaries.

One final word on employment: please do not teach your child the 'it's not my job' mindset. If we model to our children that we do what needs to be done, we don't judge work as being below us. We work alone or with others to do what is in the best interest of our home, or community, or workplace. I cleaned the bathroom at work when the custodian wasn't able to make it in and it needed to be done. If we go to work each day willing to do what needs to be done to the best of our ability, being grateful for our ability to do what we do, being a good citizen who does our best for our communities, our children will be more likely to emulate that behavior which builds better homes, workplaces, and communities. Just a thought!

LIFE BITES:

- Work is an important part of most people's lives. Just because someone is on disability doesn't mean theyu can't work. There are benefits navigators who can help determine what will happen to a disability check if someone is on disability and earns a paycheck.
- Give your child chores and allow them to do things for themselves but give them room to fail and try again.
- Believe your child has the ability to resolve problems and then give them opportunities to do so.
- Allow your children opportunities to experience disappointment and failure. Remind them these are emotions they experience; *they* are not disappointments or failures.
- Think about the needs you have for your own employment success and the skills you learn from parenting kids with challenges that help you be a better employee.

FRIENDS ARE A PRECIOUS COMMODITY

Friends improve the quality of life for all of us. In my experience, it is sometimes challenging for people with many types of disabilities to get and keep friends throughout their lives. The most heartbreaking thing for me with Alex has been his lack of friends. The few friends he did have in school got older and moved on with their lives. He now has two adult friends who are wonderful, Julian and Rocky. He loves his time with them and I am very grateful to see them having fun together. As parents, there are a few things we can do to help facilitate healthy friendships for our children.

Create opportunities that are fun for all, like a birthday party for your child, play dates, take a bunch of friends to the movies or to do something fun at your house with your child. Don't expect this to be perfect. Let go of expecting your house to be perfect, or the food or even the experience. With Alex, it can be such a challenge because his expectations are so high. He wants everything to go exactly like he wants it in his mind, but it never does. We try to help him see the good side, that it was fun and to remember to be grateful. This can help but there are times when he just wants more.

Alex can be a grateful person; if someone gives him a gift, he is grateful. But if it is an experience, it seems like it is never good enough for him. This is partly because he has mood disorder. It is common for someone with a mood disorder to feel like what is happening does not bring them joy no matter what it is. I believe another part is because he watches movies all the time so he believes his life should be like that, at least *once* in a while. We don't let this stop us from trying to give him as many positive experiences as we can but it can be frustrating.

One thing I have done is make friends with adults with disabilities and do things with them. This just happened naturally; I didn't set out to find someone with a disability to befriend. I have had two friends in my life that would fall into this category. I have had other friends with disabilities of course, but there are two whom I can't imagine my life without. They are Bob in Omaha and Paulette here in Denver. I became friends with Bob before Alex was born and Paulette when Alex was three years old. My friendship with these two individuals has taught me a great deal about people who are developmentally delayed, about having fun, being myself, and about unconditional love. It has helped Alex because he has gotten to know them and now, he can honestly say they are his friends, too.

Knowing people with disabilities before Alex was born took away some of the fear of having a child with a disability. My parents both worked in foodservice throughout their careers, including my mother who was the foodservice manager at the Nebraska School for the Deaf in Omaha. They each had employees with disabilities that I had gotten to know well and who had become good friends of our family. My friendship with Bob and his parents also took away some of the fear of having a child with a disability when Alex was born. I had a good point of reference. I knew that people with disabilities had many gifts to offer the world. I could see the possibilities in Alex, not just have the fear of the unknown.

Be grateful for your child's friends. Do what you can to foster their friendship. Take them places; open up your house to them. Let them know how grateful you are for them. Bob's mother has always been wonderful at this. She has sent me thank you letters, birthday and Christmas cards, just to express her gratitude for my friendship with Bob. This has meant so much to me over the years. It was not necessary for me to remain friends with Bob. It was just a nice gesture on her part.

One thing that can help develop friendships is if people get an opportunity to know more about your child. We made a little book about Alex since his speech is difficult to understand. This book contained information to give people a better picture of him, like what he likes to do, his favorite foods and his family. We used it to share with his teachers before he started each grade, but it can be used with new friends and other professionals, too. It helps them learn what he is like, what he enjoys doing, what his family is like, and other important details about him. I encourage you to create this for your own child, including any information you think would be helpful to a person who wants to get to know them. Shutterfly is a great online resource to help make such books for a reasonable cost or you can print off pictures and make your own book.

For people with ADD or severe allergies or medical issues, friendship can be challenging as well. One of the challenges with Alli's ADD is that she is not always good at social interactions because she doesn't read social cues well. With Alli, she has always been an individual, not afraid to be who she is, even if that isn't the 'cool' thing to be. This is one of her traits that I really admire, but it hasn't always made her the most popular person, at least in public school. But when she began her high school years at Rocky Mountain School of Expeditionary Learning, which is a school based on Outward Bounds principles that focus on character values as well as academics, she finally found a place that truly valued her for who she was. This led to many friendships for her in high school which made high school a positive experience for her.

Katy is our most social child. She has always made friends easily but when she developed her pain issues and life-threatening allergies, it made it more difficult to keep friends. She had to have friends who didn't smoke pot because of her allergy to marijuana (not easy to find in Colorado!) and she couldn't always do things like go to dances because of pain issues. The friends that stuck with her are amazing people.

I hate to even mention this but I have seen horrible things on Facebook that people have done to individuals with disabilities, so be careful! If someone wants your child to go to their house to play, have them come to your house first. Watch how they interact and make sure their motives are loving. I have also seen wonderful, loving stories on Facebook. Focus on those! Remember what we focus on we will get more of and we definitely want more loving relationships for our kids.

I also want to say a word about neighbors. Neighbors are convenient friends. They are close by and can possibly help in emergency situations. It is important to let them know a little about what is going on with your child, like if they have a habit of wandering away. Our neighbors have helped us find Alex after he has wandered away and sat with him until we find them. They can be someone to talk to if you are a stay-at-home caregiver. Remember the old days when neighbors got together to play cards on Saturday nights? That would be a great thing to do now if possible. We haven't done that yet, although I may give it a try. We do know many of our neighbors and we are lucky to be able to call them friends. They are awesome people who are always willing to help out! I hope that you can build that in your own neighborhood.

LIFE BITES:

- Friendships make life better for all of us.
- Do what you can to foster friendships for your children and to be a good friend yourself. Your quality of life depends on it!
- Get to know your neighbors and remember to be grateful for the friends and good neighbors you have.
- It's not the quantity of friends you have, but the quality of those friendships that is most important.

SIBLINGS, THE GREAT BALANCING ACT

Siblings are such an important part of who we become for all of us. Where we are in our family's birth order or if we are an only child all appear to make a difference in our personality and other characteristics we possess. It seems to me that when a sibling has a disability, the effect is even more pronounced. Depending on how the parents deal with the situation will determine if the impact creates more positive or negative characteristics. How we deal with the balancing act *matters*.

There is no doubt that your child with a disability will require more attention throughout their lives; you can't change that fact. There will be times when their siblings are jealous. What can you do to diminish the jealousy and remind all your children how special they are? One thing you can do is to be honest about what is going on with the child with the challenge and why they need the extra help. You can say it in an age-appropriate way but it is important to acknowledge it.

Let all your children know how much they are loved and valued just for being themselves. Do what you can to spend one on one time with each child even if it is only for 15 minutes before bed. Sit with them, read them a story, find out about their day, say a prayer together, whatever. Make sure it is time where your attention is just on them — no cell phone or other device. This reinforces that they are also worthy of your time and love.

If possible, include them in assisting with the child with disabilities. Maybe there is some therapy that needs to be done where they can help out. Even if it seems like a small thing to you, it helps them to feel included and needed. When you create a loving, inclusive environment for all your children, they can gain amazing insight by having a sibling with a disability. My children have great work ethics and empathy for people who are viewed as 'different.' They are creative problem solvers who can handle emergency situations. This isn't because Fred and I are wonderful parents, but because they have learned so much from each other about the value in all people and how to handle challenging situations.

There may be times when you can't balance life, like when your child is in the hospital or going through extensive treatments. There is only so much of you to go around! When this happens, ask for help. Can a trusted friend take your other child out to lunch or come over and help them with their homework or play a game? Grandparents can be a wonderful help, too. I remember when Katy was in the hospital, and I stayed with her; my mother was a huge help with Alex. We are very lucky to have had my mother to help us. If you don't have a grandparent who could help, you might reach out to a local church. If you have a Mormon church nearby, they would be a good place to start to see if they have any volunteers who can help you. I have had clients over the years who have gotten rides to doctor's appointments, clothing, and rental assistance through Mormon churches.

What do you do when your only child has special needs? Raising an only child always has challenges but when the child has a disability, it can even be more so. There are amazing people who are only children, some of whom have disabilities, like John Lennon and Brooke Shields. According to Parents magazine, here are some things that you can do to guide your only child to be their best self. As I mentioned before, help forge friendships. This is important for all children but for our kids with challenges and without siblings, it is even more critical! If they have cousins or other relatives, work on developing those relationships, too. Family has a greater chance of staying connected long term.

Allow your children to do as much for themselves as possible. Foster their independence; even if they can't do it as well as you would, encourage them to try. This is even more important for the only child because there can be a tendency to do too much for them which isn't empowering in the long run.

Be conscious of the needs of your child or children. In every situation, we can guide our children to be their best self when we let love lead and we let go of our own guilt in the situation. When we focus on our guilt and that we aren't doing enough or whatever other guilt we may be feeling, it takes away our focus from being *our* best selves.

Of course, we are going to feel guilt from time to time but the more we can forgive ourselves, or our children, or spouse or situation, the more we can focus on solutions that are centered in love, including loving ourselves! Loving ourselves is a great gift that we can give ourselves and our families. We will talk more about how to do that in the chapter on Self and Relationship Care.

Don't forget in this balancing act to give attention to your spouse occasionally, too! Keeping your relationship strong with your significant other helps in so many ways. I can't imagine life without the assistance of Fred. We can give each other breaks when we need them; we have someone who really understands what we are going through and can even laugh about it sometimes! Find people whom you trust who can watch your children even for a little bit so you can have a moment together. Make sure to spend time listening to each other about things that are unrelated to the kids. Communication is so important for healthy relationships and taking time to have a conversation together shows that you value each other.

Work toward attaining balance; let all those you love know how much they are loved and don't beat yourself up when you forget. Being hard on yourself doesn't help anything! Now that our children are grown, I have an idea of how much our family has learned from each other and how being part of our family, because of all our challenges, has created the people we are today. And you know what? I love those people!

LIFE BITES:

- Let all of your children know how valued and loved they are.
- Include siblings in the care or therapies or other work for the child with issues; this helps the siblings feel needed.
- Spend quality time with all your children when possible; when it is not possible, try to recruit friends or grandparents to help out.
- Don't forget to give attention to your spouse or life partner as well. They can easily get lost in the business of life.

MONEY MATTERS

Our relationship to money matters in our lives. It is empowering to all of our children to teach them how to have a healthy relationship with money. My first book is on money from a spiritual point of view. I was a stockbroker for 19 years and I have helped individuals with their personal finances which has taught me a great deal about money. Learning about money early can avoid many problems we can acquire as adults.

In my opinion, one of the most important things you can do for your children is to not feel the need to buy them everything they want. When we buy our children everything, we teach them to appreciate nothing. It is important for all of us to learn to tell ourselves *no* sometimes. If you allow yourself to eat dessert every time you see a dessert, that doesn't lead you down a healthy path. Allowing yourself to buy everything you want any time you see it is the same way. You will end up with lots of stuff and little appreciation for any of it. All the stuff around you (or your child) can become quite overwhelming.

There are some things you can do with your children; begin when they are young, if possible. As I mentioned in the chapter on Discipline and Employment, give your child some chores to do and an allowance. If you can't do this financially yourself, still give them some chores and have their allowance be something other than money. For instance, if they do their chores, make a chore chart, and put stickers or draw a happy face to show that they have completed the task. At the end of the week, if they have completed their chores, spend quality time with them, like take them swimming, play a game, or read together. Instill in them that being of service to others, even if it is emptying the dishwasher, has benefits. When we do something good, good things come back to us. We don't want to keep giving things to our children without them doing anything in return. That may set up an entitlement attitude, which is not empowering.

Teach your children how to spend money in healthy ways. It is more effective to teach them how to spend money before you teach them how to save money. When you take them to a store, tell them they have a set dollar amount they can spend, like $10.00. Before you go to the store, have them think about something they might want to buy and why they might want it. This begins to show them the value of money and that they can't just buy everything because they are in a store. This is great for developing self-discipline that will serve them well when they are adults.

You might also make a game where they go to the store to just look and buy nothing. They can look around the store and think about what they might want to buy. When they get home, ask them to draw a picture of what they wanted and how they would use it. After thinking about it more deeply, they may decide they really don't want it anyway, or that they do want it. But at least they will have had their first lesson in how to be intentional with spending money and not just buy things without thinking.

There were times when we couldn't buy anything for our children that was just for fun. We were lucky to be able to buy them a birthday or Christmas gift. If this is the case, you can create a wish journal for them where they draw pictures of what they want and why they want it. This begins to get them thinking about why they want things and if they are really important — another lesson in spending money with intention. If you can't afford to go to stores, you can possibly go to thrift stores, which are much cheaper, or go to garage sales. The cheapest time to go to garage sales is the last few hours of the sale. They won't have as much selection, but they will probably be in a bargaining mood with what they do have left!

Once they have some money from their allowance and have learned a little about how to spend money with intention, you can teach them to save for what they want. It can be a good idea to use a jar and have them draw a picture of what they are saving for which can be taped to the jar. Put on the picture how much they will need for the item along with some way of measuring how much they have saved. You could maybe draw a picture of a yardstick with the target amount shown in red and then each week they can count their money and mark how much they've accumulated on the yardstick. This is a visual way of showing how much something is worth and how well they are doing by saving towards the goal.

I also encouraged my children to give away something when they bought something. If we were going to the store to buy a new toy, we would have them find a toy they no longer play with and give it away. Before their birthday or other occasion when they will get lots of gifts, have them go through their room and get rid of some things to make way for the new ones. Give the items to a charity or person you know who needs them. This also can teach them the joy of giving.

LIFE BITES:

- It is important for all of us to have a healthy relationship to money.
- Give your children chores and allowance so they begin to understand the concept of getting paid to be of service and earning what they want.
- Don't buy your child everything they think they want; that teaches them to appreciate nothing. Spend quality time with them and help determine if the thing they are thinking of buying will improve the quality of their life or someone else's.
- Teaching children about thinking before they buy helps them develop the habit of spending money with intention, which will serve them well as an adult.

BEHAVIORS, NOW WHAT?

Not all people with special needs have 'behaviors' and those who do, range from mild to wild. Please don't read this chapter and be afraid or worry about the future. If behaviors happen, you will get through them. There is advice on how to stay safe and keep your child safe, which is important. But what is more important is how to stay as calm as possible and to stay in a place of love. Even if your child does have severe behaviors, remember—"This too shall pass." Alex went from having a behavior a month, to maybe one a year now and they are less severe.

Behaviors are there as a means to communicate something that feels very important to the person at the time and they don't believe they have any other way to communicate it. Remember when I said that Alex had tried to hit the vice principal at his high school with a rock? He was trying to communicate that he was overwhelmed — really, *really* overwhelmed but he didn't know how to say it. His behavior screamed *OVERWHELMED* to anyone who would listen.

Behaviors are not always as extreme as that. They are always a call for attention; something in their life needs attention. We had a behavior therapist come to our house once because Alex had fallen and refused to walk for over two months. He would just scoot around on his butt to get where he wanted to go. She told us to remove anything he cared about and make him earn it back by doing something for us. For instance, if he walked to the bathroom, he could pick out a movie. If he exercised a bit, he could eat chicken nuggets. This actually did work and got him walking, but Fred and I decided it was way too difficult to do every second of every day. It is a good idea and doable on a more limited basis or if you can start early and make it a habit.

I also believe you have to allow children the ability to decide some things for themselves. Being too controlling often backfires if the child is able to live on their own. When they get on their own, they may lack experience deciding things for themselves and make many poor decisions. Using the technique to have your children earn some things also helps to instill a work ethic which is beneficial.

The behavior therapist also suggested ignoring any behavior that you don't want to encourage. The thought is that any attention is good attention in the mind of the attention seeker. In other words, if Alex would say something like, "I want a new family" or "I'm going to hurt you," we were to completely ignore it. This works well in day-to-day life. But if the behavior is more explosive, then this approach is more difficult. You can't just ignore him if he is throwing things, hitting, or biting people or himself. If that happens, you need to step in.

Teen years are often the most difficult. When I was a job developer for people with disabilities, I worked with a super nice guy who was in his 30's and mildly developmentally delayed. He told me that when he was in his teens, he would get so angry and violent that they would have to put him in a padded room so he wouldn't hurt anyone or himself. It gave me a great deal of hope because he certainly had outgrown those types of behaviors and was able to work.

When Alex was a teenager, these types of behavior would occur in varying degrees about once a month. Now they occur about once or twice a year. There are a couple of reasons why I believe this has happened. First and foremost, he doesn't have the hormones of a teenager anymore. Secondly, he no longer has to go to school or to a day program every day. The process of getting him ready and out of the house daily was the cause of about 60% of his behaviors. Now he gets to hang out at home with dad which has been helpful. And lastly, he is on a new medicine from the doctor and I give him niacin and vitamin D which has definitely helped improve his mood. Do be careful of niacin flush if you try niacin. That is when you get too much niacin and your skin gets itchy and you feel hot. Google it and talk to a health care professional before starting any supplements.

Here are some things we have learned when it gets extreme:

1. One of the things that may cause Alex to explode is when he doesn't get to do something. Going to see a movie in the

movie theater can be a trigger for him. For instance, if the movie has a romantic element, Alex will want very much to have a girlfriend. One time, we were leaving the theater after such a movie. Alex saw a pretty girl and asked her if she would marry him. Of course, she said no.

That got Alex *very* angry. He threw his glasses and then spiraled into a behavior where he wouldn't leave the lobby of the theater. He threw his shoes and hit me. There were two police officers there, thank goodness. They restrained him and since Alex had not started to calm down even after 20 minutes, they called for an ambulance. On the ambulance, they were able to give him some meds to help calm him down, but it still took a couple hours in the emergency room before he was back to himself. It is very interesting to note that, after such an incident, it seems like someone flipped a switch in his brain that resets him. Once he 'resets,' he is remorseful about his behavior and will often call himself a monster which is heartbreaking for us.

When you figure out the triggers, then you can do what you can to avoid them. Now we are careful about the movies Alex goes to and Fred takes him in the morning when there are fewer people at the theater so there is less chance of a problem occurring.

2. If your child explodes into a behavior, do whatever you can to keep yourself calm and *NOT* angry! They will feed off whatever energy you are putting out. If we have to restrain Alex, I always tell him that I love him. He usually screams back, "No, you don't!" but that doesn't stop me.

3. If we notice that Alex is beginning to escalate (sometimes there is no warning), I will sing "Hu" quietly, close to him. Hu is the ancient word for God; I sing it at around middle C. It is amazing how it can change the energy in the room to a more loving, positive energy. Just doing this has avoided some behaviors. There are several Youtube videos about singing the Hu. I encourage you to watch them to learn more. I will also send Alex blessings quietly so he doesn't hear it, like: "Alex, I send you blessings of love. I send you blessings that you will

let go of all negative emotions, you will not resist your life, but you will let your life flow." If there is more than one person in the room, one can sing Hu while the other sends blessings. It is so important that they feel you love them unconditionally. We don't want our children to feel like monsters!

4. If you have to restrain the person because they are causing harm to themselves, someone else, or their surroundings, try to do these things:

- Take off your glasses, earrings, or necklace that can be grabbed and used to hurt you, or things that are expensive to replace if they break.
- Do whatever you can to keep your cell phone on you in a pants pocket or other place — out of reach for your child — at all times which can be used to call for help.
- Remove large objects that are close and can be thrown which would be dangerous.
- If there is more than one person involved and the situation is not calming down, call 911. Of course, you can call 911 if you are alone, too; it just may be more difficult. There is an app called Emergency SOS you can get on your iPhone so you can quickly call the emergency number.
- Restraining Alex seems to allow him to get rid of some of his emotions through his physical exertion trying to fight us off. Once he has calmed down, which you can tell because he will start crying and his body will relax, he seems to be much calmer than even before the event.
- There are different types of restraints you can use; it can be hard to think about things you have learned when you are in such a situation. The most important thing to do is do what you can to keep their arms and legs from moving so getting them down on the ground, hopefully face down, is important. Also keeping away from their head, which they can use to hit or bite you, is preferable. You can learn about different types of restraints from Youtube which may be helpful.

5. If the police do come, that doesn't mean that charges will be filed, at least that is the case in our community. The police have been wonderful to us; they help calm Alex down and make sure we are safe. It is very important to have a lock on the knife drawer in your kitchen and to make sure any knives, guns, or other weapons are locked and completely out of reach. If a police officer comes into your home and someone is wielding a weapon (which actually can be almost anything if they are using it in a threatening way), they have to do whatever is necessary to keep themselves and others safe.

It is possible to have some post traumatic stress from dealing with behaviors. You can live in a place of fear, wondering what will happen next. It may help to release some of those feelings by focusing on forgiveness. Forgive your child for their behavior, possibly forgive yourself for how you handled the situation, and let it go. This is much easier said than done, but definitely a worthy goal that will help you live from a place of love instead of fear.

With behaviors like your child trying to hurt you, it is easy to feel shame as a parent for raising a child who would do that. Know that all of us feel shame about something. Shame is different from guilt. Guilt says, "I did something bad;" shame says, "I am bad." Maybe you feel shame because you got angry at your child and didn't handle it as well as you could, or maybe you feel shame because you have to go to work with a black eye that your child gave you.

Sometimes I would have to go to work two or three hours late, still crying because of the trauma of that morning's behavior and waiting for the police to come. I felt shame walking through the door to work, having to admit my child's behavior through my tears. It was awful! I was grateful though that I worked at Bayaud which is a non-profit agency that works with people with disabilities. They understood. My boss had a mother with schizophrenia, so he understood; he even understood the shame piece. When you feel shame, I am assuming you will at one point or another, talk with another parent who has a chance of understanding. There is no handbook for parenting in general and sure as hell no handbook for how to deal with your child's behaviors! Do the best that you can to love yourself and your child through these times. Know that if you can do that, or close to that, you will gain the hard lessons that come from this time. Know there are lessons there and this, too, shall pass!

Make sure to talk to the other people who were involved in the behavior, like siblings, your spouse, friends, whoever, so that together, everyone can sort through their feelings to have a healthier outcome and let go of negative emotions, like shame, blame and anger.

LIFE BITES:

- Don't let the fear of behaviors stop you from doing things but use common sense. As I mentioned before I am not going to take Alex to a movie about a love story or take him when the theater will be crowded.
- Think about what the person may be trying to communicate through the behavior.
- Remember to send blessings, sing Hu, keep as much love in the situation as possible, and if needed, call the police.
- You will get through this time; just make sure to reach out for help when you need it and remember "This too shall pass." I told you that would come in handy!

THE IMPORTANCE OF SEXUALITY

Sexuality is an important part of who we are. Teaching our children about their own sexuality, their bodies, and to listen to their gut may keep them from being sexually abused. Teaching them to respect sex and themselves may also guide them to develop a healthy concept of sex in this world where that can be hard to find.

If you want your child to have a healthy relationship with their sexuality, respect them enough to be honest about their bodies. Don't call your son's penis or your daughter's vagina their 'private parts' or 'unmentionables' or whatever; use the correct terms. Teach them that they control their body and the space around them. They are in control of who is allowed to touch them and that they should ask before touching someone else. Don't tell them that and then turn around and make them hug Aunt Ethel or Uncle Bob. They can choose if they want to hug or be hugged by someone. Individuals with cognitive disabilities are more likely to be sexually assaulted; this is one thing you can do to help prevent that. Knowledge is so important!

Another thing that is important to teach your children is to trust their gut. If something doesn't feel right, trust that feeling regardless of who is causing them to feel that way. Even if it is a doctor or relative or teacher or preacher, if they are touching them in a way that makes them feel uncomfortable, let them know they have to right to leave, and then tell you about it. Listen to your children if they say something happened. Make sure to hear both sides of the story, too; it is possible that there was something legitimate going on that your child didn't understand. Keep your eyes and ears open to determine the truth of the situation. People who abuse others are manipulative and skilled at hiding what is really going on.

Allow your daughters to define themselves in ways that encompass all of who they are, not just that they are 'pretty.' Encourage learning, trying new things, solving problems, etc. and allow them to define themselves however they choose, and celebrate that. My parents called me 'pumpkin' and didn't emphasize my looks. They told me I was smart and had good ideas. That has served me well as an adult. It is also fine to let them know they are beautiful. They can be smart and beautiful!

When your children are in their preteen or teenager years, they will masturbate (yes, I said it and yes it will happen). Teach them that it is something they need to do when they are alone, and they can do it in their room or other private place at home. This is a natural part of life and not something to feel ashamed about. Releasing some sexual energy is important for all of us.

If your child will be having sex at some point with others, teach them about birth control. I would say that if your child can be home alone for two or more hours or they can go to someone else's house without you or another caregiver, there is a possibility they will be sexually active at some point. Tell your daughters about the pill or other birth control that you and your doctor deem appropriate. For your son, teach them about condoms. Show them how to use them. Teach them to respect women and to listen when a woman says "No." Anytime they talk about kissing someone, make sure to remind them that they have to ask first.

Our son loves pretty girls. He watches them and often goes up to them and either asks them to dance, get married, or go on a date. He does understand that he needs to ask them before hugging or kissing them which is good. My husband had a brilliant idea for Alex. He made him business cards with roses on them and Alex's name and email address. Alex can give a card to girls he is interested in so they can contact him. He can give this card to any woman or girl he wishes. It is like giving her a rose with his contact information. It usually works well with Alex; he can give it to her and then move on. The sad thing is no one has ever emailed him, but that goes with the chapter on friends. The good thing is Alex really doesn't think about it again so he hasn't noticed that no one has emailed him.

I teach a sex education class to a group of adults with disabilities. It is more effective to have this discussion using pictures of sexual organs which can be found in books or on the internet; just be careful what you google! A great resource I have used is Planned Parenthood. They have great information on sex education specifically for parents, even parents of kids with special needs, which you can look up. Opening up the conversation about sex with our children is important for their health and safety. It may be a bit uncomfortable, so use a little humor. Let them know that this may not be super comfortable but that it is super important.

As a parent, I feel keeping the lines of communication open on this important topic may empower our children to talk more freely with us about all aspects of sex and sexuality. Allow them to ask you questions, any question. This may help keep our children safe. One way to share with your children about sex is to remind them that sex is sacred, an incredible gift from Spirit where two beings intertwine and share their energies. Make sure that whoever you give access to your body to is someone worthy of getting some of your energy and someone whose energy you want to get.

Young people experiment with their bodies and want to explore other's bodies sexually because it is a natural part of being human. We all do it. Don't teach them shame, but how to honor their bodies and the bodies of others, to be comfortable with their bodies, and to understand that sex is a gift not to be abused. Advise them to do what they do out of mutual respect and love and to enjoy the process.

One of my daughter's friends shared with me that her parents hadn't taught her anything about sex or contraception. This was when she was 19 years old and entering college. She was dating a man who was her first sexual partner. He had told her that he didn't need to use condoms and that she wouldn't get pregnant. She believed him and continued this unhealthy relationship for quite a while.

I understand that for her parents this conversation is uncomfortable. But I think we would all agree that it is important to have some control over what our children are taught about sex, so they understand the facts. Having no information is scary. Just using Google or your friends can lead you down paths of inaccurate information that may even be dangerous.

Be open and honest about sex. Use correct words for body parts. Teach your children that they control their own bodies at all times, even if it is a trusted professional like a teacher, doctor or preacher or family friend who makes them feel uncomfortable. If someone makes them feel uncomfortable, allow them to talk about it with you. Don't judge them; allow them to speak openly. Get help through a counselor or other professionals if you feel they have been sexually violated. If you have been sexually violated as a child and never sought help, it is not too late. Find a trusted professional to talk to about it. You are worth it and so are your children!

LIFE BITES:

- The conversation about sex is not always comfortable but it is always important.
- Be honest with your children about sex, their bodies, and sexuality.
- Teach them to trust their gut and to let someone know if someone has done something that makes them feel uncomfortable.
- Teach them that sex is a sacred gift which is why it is important to respect their bodies and the bodies of others.
- You may not catch everything and always be able to keep your children safe, like when I didn't realize Alli was cutting herself. Instead of beating yourself up, send blessings that whatever happens will hold some lesson that will allow your child to grow and learn something of value, and be there to love them no matter what.
- Seek help if you feel you or your child has been sexually violated.

HUMOR! A SURVIVAL TOOL

Thank goodness my husband and I had a sense of humor. I'm pretty sure that without it, we would not have stayed married for almost 40 years before he passed away. Being able to laugh at ourselves and our situation released so much tension and allowed us to stay more positive.

There was an article in the Denver Post on August 28, 2016 about a poet named Max Ritvo who had dealt with cancer from his childhood until his death at age 25. His book, which is available on Amazon, is called *Four Reincarnations*. Here is a quote from the newspaper article that I think is helpful to us as parents.

> "Ritvo saw humor not as a coping mechanism but as an intrinsic part of dealing with his illness. "You know, we imagine in our hysteria that it's disrespectful for the sadness. But when you laugh at something horrible, you're just illuminating a different side of it that was already there and it's not a deflection, it makes it deeper and makes it realer."

Max's attitude was inspirational. According to his wife, he said, "I love you" to everyone. He just wanted there to be more love and laughter. I believe that for many individuals living with disabilities or medical issues, this is true. They show us how to love, laugh, and be real.

My family has certainly given me many things to laugh about. Sometimes these are little things that make us laugh, like when Alex tells us we're giving him a heart attack! Or when we try to hand him his dinner only to have him say, "I'm not hungry enough for *that*!" or accuse us of trying to feed him weeds when I gave him kale.

Sometimes they are more involved situations, like the time before Katy went in for surgery when she asked her anesthesiologist if he had watched a Youtube video on the procedure so he would make sure to get it right. Thank goodness, he had a sense of humor. There was also the time when Alli and Katy were spending the night at their grandmother's house. They were in bed, trying to sleep. Katy had been staring at the fire alarm when Alli let out a fart that was so loud Katy was convinced it was the fire alarm which scared the crap out of her! She jumped out of bed and woke up her grandma so they could all quickly leave the house. Alli had to reassure them that it was just her loud flatulence so they could calm down and go back to sleep.

When Alex was about eight years old, he broke his arm. He went to bed in a cast but when he woke up in the morning, it was off. At that time, Fred worked at night, and I worked during the day. Fred had to call me to check and see if Alex had gotten the cast off which, of course, he hadn't. He had just escaped from it.

The most work we have ever done for the sake of humor was creating a Barney video spoof. This is because Alex watches lots of Barney videos and owns almost all of them. In our spoof, Barney is enjoying a cigarette and beer with his friend, Winnie the Pooh, after a hard day of filming. We had Barney trying to pick up Barbie and all kinds of other shenanigans. The afternoon of creating that video was probably the most I have ever laughed in one afternoon. It turned out great; too bad it was before Youtube and we have since lost it so you won't get the pleasure of watching it. Creating funny videos is a great afternoon activity if you want to perk things up a bit!

Don't be afraid to laugh. Make sure that you aren't making fun of someone; instead, that you are making fun with someone. There is a big difference. Making fun with someone has the motivation of sharing love and joy. In our house, laughing is one of our strong suits and I'm so grateful it is!

LIFE BITES:

- Don't be afraid to laugh!
- Remember that laughter is just illuminating a different side of what is already there.
- Laughter has the power to get us through our day-to-day challenges in ways that help us see the lesson and reduce our stress.

SPIRITUAL LIFE

Be open. Breathe. Take in a new breath, a new thought. Does it reflect love? Expansion? Possibility?

For people whose mind works differently, it is quite possible that their thoughts around spirituality and religion may also be more open. For those of us whose religious upbringing was more traditional or strict, this may be challenging. You may feel the need to pull them back in, lest they fall to the dark side.

I encourage you, before you try to dissuade them—listen. Ask yourself the above questions. Is what they're sharing coming from a place of love? Expansion? Possibility? Be open. I'm not saying that you will believe everything they say; I am just saying to really listen.

Alli, our oldest daughter, has always had a problem of going to church. It never felt comfortable, accepting, or loving to her even though to me, it was an open and progressive Methodist church. I didn't make her go. This was challenging because when I was growing up, my brothers and I were one of two places on Sunday morning: either at church or dead (ok, maybe not dead, but at least feeling like we were on our death bed)! It served me well. I loved going to church, singing in the choir, and everything else. But I am also grateful that my parents allowed me to ask questions about any and everything. I did, and still do, question.

Later, when Alli announced that she was Wiccan, I had to be open. I had to ask her questions as to what that meant. Then I was able to embrace her decision. She would have done it whether or not I accepted it. But my accepting it allowed me to learn from it, grow through it, and celebrate her growth on her journey to become Wiccan. The Wiccan religion has more of a focus on reverence for nature and the worship of gods and goddesses. Alli has taken me to some of the rituals. It has deepened my appreciation of Mother Earth and the world around me.

It has shown me about embracing both the masculine and the feminine, the light and the dark that resides in all of us. I'm now grateful for her decision. I'm also grateful for my mother's (her only living grandparent) acceptance of it at the time.

Alex went to church as a child but seldom has gone as an adult. This is partly because of his behaviors. Often, when he does go, he wants to get married that day to whatever pretty girl has caught his eye. I know you will find this hard to believe, but it's hard to find a young girl ready for that kind of commitment on a Sunday morning! But Alex's understanding of God or Source or the Universe or whatever you want to call it, is deep! When Alex was about nine years old, we were doing our bedtime ritual, which was reading a book, saying a prayer, and then I would sing a little song. After we said the prayer, he told me that God was soft and warm and that God always loved him. Another time, as we were waiting to get on a plane when he was in his early 20's, he looked around at the 60 or so people waiting to board. He told me, "God loves everyone here." I believe that one of the gifts of people who are developmentally delayed is that they haven't put up the walls around their heart that separate them from God or Source. They understand love in a beautifully simple way.

For Katy, she has always loved church, the people, the lessons, the thoughts. This has served her well. I am grateful she does question what she is learning; she thinks about it before just accepting it. I believe that is such an important part of our own spiritual growth — being free to question, to think. It is much healthier than being spoon fed our religion. My parents allowed me to question freely as a child. I have continued this as an adult which has led me to learn about various religious and spiritual practices. One of the most powerful spiritual practices I have learned is about sending blessings which I described more in the chapter on Letting Go.

One of the gifts our children bring is their ability to see the world differently through open eyes that don't have all the preconceived notions that the rest of us may have. They can also be more open to receive what others give to them — like when Alex was having the behavior and people stopped to help us. When we allowed them to assist us, we accepted gratefully the gift they were giving us. This allowed grace to move through the situation, opening the door for them to be the hero. They were able to give to another from a place of love without expecting anything in return. I know they felt as good about helping us as we felt about receiving their assistance.

The fact that our kids need help at times gives another person the opportunity to *be* love and to receive love. I believe this is one of children's greatest gifts. Having a behavior can seem like the farthest thing from love, but it certainly gives us a moment to exercise our own love muscle and a moment for someone else to be a hero! What a gift and what a lesson in spirituality!

LIFE BITES:

- Be open. Allow space for a new thought, a new idea based on love.
- Listen. Give your children freedom to be the love that they are.
- Learn from your children; they truly can be great teachers!

PRECIOUS TIME

The time we have with our children is precious. It goes quickly. The truth is none of us know how much time we will have on this earth together. There are many disabilities that can cause life to be even more brief. Alex has Down syndrome, severe sleep apnea, and diabetes — none of which help with longevity. Katy has already faced death once when she was intubated for three days because of an allergic reaction to fish. It was one of those times when I literally got on my knees and gave it up to God — the worry, the fear. It was when I realized the power of releasing our fears to Source. I don't believe that the prayer put God into action, but it did open *me* up to the grace flowing through me which allowed me to find the lesson or gift in my own journey. It opened me up to the love of God which is always there — that love that can carry us through all of life.

Katy did recover, but not all children do. My nephew, John, and his wife Julie's four-year-old son, Carson, who had Down syndrome, didn't survive even though his parents had said the same prayer. Releasing our concerns to God means being able to accept the outcome, knowing that we can find some lesson in it all as we lean into God's love. In Carson's short life, he taught all of us about love and gratitude. All he knew in his life was love. He has wonderful parents and brothers and sisters who showed him only love. He experienced more love in those four years than some people do in 90 years.

We don't know all the mysteries of life and the whys. But if we allow it, our children can help us see that there is a gift in it all, that we can use the challenges in our lives to guide us to becoming the people our souls want us to be, to learn the lessons we are here to learn. Whatever time we have with our children is precious and a great gift. In the day-to-day struggles of it all, try not to forget that.

What if we choose to see it all as perfect? Our kids, their challenges, behaviors, gifts, the love they show us? How would it change the energy around our time with them? Maybe we could just be with it, accept it all for the gift it is — release our need to be what society calls the 'perfect' parent and instead understand our role as co-creators and caregivers, to guide our children to be their best self as we accept their guidance directing us to be our best self. Maybe instead of that feeling of dread in the pit of our stomach that worries, "What's next?" we could live at ease, knowing that whatever is next is meant to be and it will bring some gift, some lesson that is just what we need even when it doesn't feel like it.

There is a life changing quote from Eckhart Tolle that goes, 'Whatever the present moment contains, accept it as if you had chosen it. Always work with it, not against it.' This has helped me a great deal, not only with dealing with my children, but also with the individuals experiencing homelessness that I worked with every day. It helps me to stay positive and always on the look out for the gift.

Once we are a parent to a special needs child, we will always be, whether our child is still in the physical world or not. Raising all children should be a community effort, but raising children with special challenges makes getting assistance from others in the community imperative. There is always an opportunity to participate in the raising of other special children, whether it is giving requested advise over the phone, watching the child to give the parent a break, or other help. We are much more successful doing this parenting thing together. I remember a mother from church who had a special needs child, taking all three of my children after church one day so I could get a break. It meant the world to me!

Being a caregiver to our children, regardless of their age, can easily become how we define ourselves. When they pass, it can be even more difficult because we not only lose our child, but also our role as caregiver — really our identity. There is a tendency to feel lost if this happens. Make sure to reach out and get the help you need to walk through the grief and all the changes in your life.

Grief is a powerful emotion and one that we need to allow ourselves to feel and work through. We need to recognize that children also feel grief; so do people who are not able to verbalize their thoughts. Every one of us has the capability to feel grief. Acknowledging this is important. Writing a letter to the person who has passed and then burning it safely to send the message on is a technique that may help someone deal with grief. If your child can't write by themselves, you can do this by asking them questions to find out what they want to say. Looking at pictures with them and talking about the person and what they miss may also be helpful.

One time, I worked for a company as a job developer, but they also offered in-home care to people with disabilities and the elderly. This particular day, they had no one to watch a woman whose mother had recently passed away so they asked me to do it. I watched her for an afternoon but I could sense her sadness. She was mobile but non-verbal with developmental disability. I talked to her about how she must be feeling sad because of her mother's passing. Even though she couldn't respond verbally, it seemed that acknowledging her pain and that it was normal at least gave her a little validation.

My nephew, John, decided to write a blog that has chronicled his grief journey. One of the things he said was that grief has an energy of its own. It can either drag you down or you can use it to move you forward to do amazing things. He decided to participate in an Ironman Boulder triathlon. He put the names of other children who had passed on his bike to carry their memory into the future. It was a way for him to make sense of the grief and move forward as much as possible. Life will never be the same, but there is a way to go on living. His blog, if you would like to check it out, is http://daddingashardasican.blogspot.com/

Recognize the precious time we have here together. Don't take it for granted! Use it to connect with those around you and show your love. We have been given a sacred responsibility; may we do it to the best of our ability!

LIFE BITES:

- Remember how precious our time together is and cherish it; don't take it for granted.
- The quote from Eckhart Tolle, "Whatever the present moment contains, accept it as if you had chosen it. Always work with it, not against it."
- Allow yourself to feel grief and give yourself time to work through it. There is no right or wrong way to grieve and no time limit.

SELF AND RELATIONSHIP CARE

Children benefit when we model how to keep ourselves healthy and have healthy, happy relationships. Self care to me means doing things that keep you healthy and give you a little breathing room so you don't get too overwhelmed to deal with day-to-day life.

I believe that the best gift we can give our children, as well as ourselves, our families, and communities, is to love ourselves. When we love ourselves, we are gentle with the self-talk in our heads. We can let go of our need to criticize our every move and instead be more loving and encouraging to ourselves. Think about your self-talk. If you told your best friend that it was your spouse or partner who said those words to you instead of your self-talk, what would they say? Would they tell you the person is abusive and you should get away from them or would they say how lucky you are to be in such a loving relationship? Start to develop that loving relationship by being kind. Talk to yourself like you would to you as a 5-year-old child. No need to be so hard on yourself; it serves no one. Start where you can and keep working on it because you are worth it!

When we love ourselves, we also know we are worthy of good things happening to us. We don't let people just take advantage of us. We make more empowering choices which are better for us and all those around us. It is also where true joy originates. In the book *Conversations with God*, Neal Donald Walsch says that true happiness comes from three things: knowing ourselves, being ourselves, and loving ourselves.

Here are some suggestions that have worked for me and my family to help show not only our love for ourselves, but how to create and model great self-care.

You must take time for yourself. For me, it is good for my well-being to go out with friends occasionally just for fun. Also, once a year,

I go on a women's spiritual retreat and an annual girls weekend with my daughters and mother. It is important during this time to not feel guilty that you are gone, but to really enjoy the time even if that means just sitting and reading a book. For Fred, he volunteered to be a corner worker at various car races. He would leave on Friday night and come back on Sunday. He would just go and enjoy it, not worrying about what is going on at home. It is a time for each of us to recharge our batteries. This makes us better parents and caregivers the rest of the year.

I have a daily practice of getting up early in the morning to meditate and do qi gong, pronounced chee-gong. I have been meditating for a little over four years and doing qi gong for over thirteen years. There are lots of great guided meditations or just meditation music available on Youtube, which I use, or you can just sit and listen to something like a fan. The form of qi gong I practice is called Spring Forest Qi Gong, which you can also find on Youtube. I do this for 15 minutes a day. This daily practice gives me energy and focus, helps me let go of stress, and lets me achieve better health.

If it is difficult for you to find time to add something extra to your day, then wash your hands mindfully. Every time you wash your hands, feel your feet grounded into Mother Earth. Notice how the water feels as it washes over your hands and how the soap smells. Feel grateful for all your hands allow you to do and how washing your hands helps you and those you love stay healthy. Look in the mirror and say, "I love you." Relax into the moment. This is a great way to bring calmness and love into your life without requiring more of a time commitment.

Take time together as a couple. This can be just going out to breakfast or lunch or going to a movie or on a walk. It can even be just sitting in a room away from the kids and having a conversation. It is important to remember to do this. It is something we really have to focus on or it easily gets forgotten. I am lucky to have had a loving and supportive partner like Fred but it can be easy to take relationships for granted. They take focus and work and they are never perfect but they should be good more often than not with a focus on guiding each other to be the best we can be.

Keep a sense of humor. As I mentioned in the chapter on humor, our senses of humor have definitely helped us go through some tough times and stay together. If you, yourself, aren't funny, at least watch some funny Youtube videos or movies together. There are some really funny things out there! Remember to find the funny!

Fight well. There was a report many years ago on national public radio about the qualities of a healthy relationship. It stated that one of the most important qualities was the ability to fight well. If you are one of those couples who say you never fight, that isn't always healthy either. If you never fight because someone is always giving in and never getting their needs met, that is not healthy. This study said that when you fight, remember these four things:

1. Stick to the issue at hand; don't bring up old issues that aren't relevant right now.
2. No name calling! You may be fighting or arguing, but you still love each other. Name calling just makes the other person feel badly, and doesn't resolve anything.
3. Take a few minutes or more to calm down before beginning the fight. This allows you to think a little more clearly before saying something you can't take back. When the fight is over, allow the next day to start with a clean slate. Don't hold grudges.
4. Make sure to really listen to each other.

The old adage to never go to bed angry is also a good one. Work through issues if possible so you don't stew on them and make them worse. Resolve them so you can move on.

Be grateful. Let your significant other know that you are grateful that they just took out the trash or put away the dishes or whatever. Let them know you are grateful that you are in this life together. Be kind and grateful as much as you can; it will take you far. I keep a daily gratitude journal where I write down the things for which I am grateful. Katy and her husband, Kevin, write in a gratitude journal together each night. Focusing on things we are grateful for brings into our lives more for which to be grateful. Remember, we will get more of whatever we focus on, so focus on the good in all things!

LIFE BITES:

- Healthy and happy relationships take work, intention, and a sense of humor.
- Take time to care for yourself each day. Even if all you do is to wash your hands mindfully, being grateful for how it keeps you healthy and for all your hands can do — that is a great start! Remember to also tell yourself, "I love you," as you look into the mirror.
- Take time together as a couple.
- Fight well, no name calling, stick to the issue at hand, listen to each other, and then resolve the issue before going to sleep.
- Don't forget to practice, practice, practice!

DISABILITY SPECIFIC INFORMATION

Here's what I have learned from my kids about each of their various diagnoses:

Attention Deficit Disorder, ADD:

The name attention deficit disorder is a little misleading. In the world according to Alli, she doesn't lack attention; she has a hard time focusing on one thing because her attention is on everything around her. Because of this, it can be helpful to keep the environment the same as much as possible. When a child with ADD is in a classroom where the room arrangement and desk location changes often, it can be very distracting because they focus on it so much.

Having such a global focus can make things like cleaning your room difficult. I remember when I would ask Alli to clean her room; the first thing she would do is empty all her drawers. I couldn't care less if she cleaned out her drawers, but because she had such a global focus to her, 'clean your room' meant clean *everything* in the room which included the drawers. It can be helpful to write out a list of what needs to be done and where to start; you can even have them help create the list. You would add things like: Put your clothes in the dirty clothes basket, put your toys in the toy box, and make your bed — specific things that they can check off as they accomplish them. Once finished, you can take pictures of the room so they can easily see next time if they have completed everything.

There is a great video that I watched many years ago called F.A.T. City. It is now on Youtube as 'How Difficult Can This Be? The F.A.T. City Workshop.' It is a glimpse into what it is like to have a learning disability. It helped me begin to understand what life is like for Alli and Fred. It talks about how difficult it can be for a child with ADD to learn to read because they move the letters on the page and how challenging it can be for them to process information especially when they feel stressed or rushed. They usually visualize what they are reading, like when they read the word, 'cat,' they picture a cat in their mind. But when they read something like 'the,' there is no mental picture for it which can make it difficult for them. You can have them create a picture for the words like 'the' which may help them.

I also know how intelligent Fred and Alli are and when they are taught in ways that make sense to them, there is no limit to what they can learn. There are new ways of teaching reading now which can be helpful, like the Lindamood-Bell approach or other new approaches to reading. History has shown us the amazing creative ability of people with ADD or ADHD (Attention Deficit Hyperactivity Disorder). Some examples of historic figures with these learning disabilities are Walt Disney and Albert Einstein, to name a few.

If you have a child with any learning disability, I highly recommend you watch the Youtube video mentioned above. It gives a better understanding of their world and how you can interact with them in ways that will be more beneficial and less frustrating. There are many books on the subject as well. *The Gift of Dyslexia*, by Ronald D. Davis was one that I read that was very helpful. This book talks about the challenges, but also the gifts of having dyslexia which he says is part of ADD and ADHD.

Severe Allergies and other medical issues:

I have learned a couple things from Katy's challenges. One is to not let fear stop you! When Katy was 16 years old, she went to New York City for two weeks by herself. Katy has severe allergies to marijuana and all types of fish. She stayed with a classmate's grandmother whom she had never met. She went all over the city, mostly by herself. She wasn't stupid; she avoided restaurants where they serve lots of fish. She didn't take other unnecessary chances but she didn't just sit inside the apartment either! She learned she could do things on her own and not live in fear.

The other major thing she has taught me is to appreciate life and let the people you love know that you love them. None of us have an expiration date stamped on our forehead. Live each day as fully as possible, being present. This allows us to live in the moment which gives us an opportunity to listen to others and to really live.

I am also grateful that we researched other forms of healing, from acupuncture, supplements, essential oils, energy healing, emotion code releases, etc. Our health is based on more than just our physical health, including our emotional health. When we look at healing anything in our lives, or even lessening symptoms, we need to address not only the physical element, but the emotional one as well.

In the book, *Emotional Agility*, by Susan David, PhD, there is a helpful exercise in releasing emotions. The exercise was created by James Pennebaker, a professor at the University of Texas. In this activity, you set a timer for 20 minutes. Write about your emotional experiences from whenever you choose — could be today or years ago. Just keep writing without regard for neatness, spelling, or punctuation. Allow your mind to take you where it will and just keep writing. Once you are done, you can throw the paper away, or do whatever you want with it; no one will ever need to see it. This allows you to write freely without worrying about other people's judgments. Do this 20-minute exercise for three days. I have done it and found it to be very freeing. Doing this exercise can help you with the emotional piece of your health.

Life with a service dog, written by Katy:

Having a service dog is both one of the most rewarding and annoying experiences of my life. When most people think of service dogs, they think they are for individuals who are blind or in wheelchairs. It is true that they are quite helpful in these areas, but they are also amazing and can do many other things. My dog smells for the allergies I have. He has saved my life more times than I can count. When you have severe airborne allergies, it can be hard to live every day and not fear dying. Having my service dog has given me strength and courage. This means he acts differently from how people assume a service dog should act. He is always smelling and moving around me to make sure that I am safe. Service dogs are a part of their person; when we work together, we are one. Having a service animal is like having an extension of yourself.

Being a person who does not look like she has a disability means that people are always asking me questions that they are afraid to ask someone who is blind or looks disabled. I have been in a Starbucks with headphones on, working on my computer, and have had people come up and ask me questions about my dog. This would be the annoying part. Just because you see a cute dog does not mean you need to talk to it. I have had people come up to me in grocery stores and tell me how wonderful I am for training service dogs. I wish people would understand that if a dog has a vest on, they are working. It is not an invitation. It does not mean I always want to talk to you. It does mean that they are working. It does mean that they are helping to make someone's life better.

I hope the next time you see a cute dog with a vest on, you still admire them but also realize that they have a job and no matter what it is, it is important.

Down Syndrome:

People with Down syndrome are accomplishing more and more these days. Have expectations that your child can accomplish things; give them the opportunity to do so. The other side of that coin is to accept them for who they are and what they can and can't do. No matter how high or low functioning (not my favorite terms) they are, see their unique perfection. They are the only one who can bring their unique gift to the world which is true for all of us.

Listen to them; let them know they matter. If it is difficult to understand their speech, ask them to say it in a different way or draw a picture of what they're saying or have them show you, if possible. Keep with them until you understand what they're saying. I remember one day it took Alex an entire day to tell us he wanted to watch Snow White. Some movie names are hard to pronounce, like Despicable Me, or Cinderella. There is also assistive technology that may help, or notebooks with pictures that they can point to, indicating what they want to say. Ask a speech therapist for assistance.

Give them control over what you appropriately can within reason and age — like maybe the choice of two different things to eat, or that they need to either empty the dishwasher, or take a shower before they get to go do something fun. We are now using a board with Alex where he gets to choose what he wants to do that day, including some chore or 'work' and some things that are fun. So far it has worked well; now I hope we keep doing it!

Try to offer a variety of foods and activities. People with Down syndrome can be a bit stubborn and stuck in their ways, so the more we offer them variety throughout their childhoods, hopefully the more open they will remain to new foods and experiences as they age.

There can be various medical issues for people with Down syndrome. Don't spend your time worrying about this but if you do notice something doesn't seem right, contact your doctor. There are entire books on this if you want to research it further.

Mood Disorder:

Mood disorder and anxiety show up in Alex as fear of the unknown and anger when things don't go his way. He can be very anxious about going into a room that he isn't familiar with or one that is full of people. He can sit outside of the room for long periods of time before he feels comfortable enough to go in, or sometimes he won't go in at all. Another way this shows up for Alex is that there are times when no matter what we do for him, it is never enough. For instance, most of the time when he goes to a movie, at the end, he is always a bit upset because it wasn't as good as he thought it would be, or he wants his life to be like the one in the movie.

The anger he shows at times can be extreme and triggered by seemingly small events. There is a drug that he takes to help stabilize his moods. When he is having a really difficult time, we also have a little happy pill that we can give him which calms him down and usually puts him to sleep.

Type 1 Diabetes:

Alex has had diabetes since he was nine years old. If you have a child with type 1 diabetes, know that you will be able to learn all you need to know and you will not always be able to keep his blood sugars within normal range. That is the first fact you need to know. It can be quite challenging to figure out how various foods, activity, stress, and illness will affect blood sugars. Do your best. Get in the habit of doing certain things, like writing down how much insulin was given after you give it and then putting the syringe away. Be in the habit of carrying your kit with you at least most of the time. School nurses must be very particular about meds. Be kind; it's not their fault!

Having high or low blood sugars makes you feel grumpy, jittery, sweaty, or clammy — in other words, not good. Make sure to check blood sugars if they are acting weird, angry for no reason, or just out of it. If it is because of blood sugars, do what you need to do to help it. If numbers are high—then they need insulin according to your doctor's instructions, if their blood sugars are low, which is below 70— then juice or frosting. Check with your doctor about more specific information about your child when their blood sugars are outside the normal range. Alex's blood sugars are rarely low, and when they are, we have raised them simply by a small glass of orange juice or some chicken nuggets. You will learn when it is an emergency situation — at which time you call 911. We have not had to call 911 for Alex because of blood sugars.

You can call the non-emergent police number in your area and tell them about the medical issues of any family member. You can also let them know about mental health issues in the household so they know to send someone who has been trained to deal with that type of crisis. We let them know that Alex has Down syndrome, diabetes and that his speech is difficult to understand. Call every year or so to make sure that the information is still accurate.

When you fill the syringe with insulin, make sure to put air into the syringe for the amount of insulin you need; shoot it into the insulin bottle and then draw up the insulin. For instance, if you need 20 units of Humalog, here are your steps:

1. Take your empty syringe and in the air pull the thumb plunger up to the 20-unit mark.
2. Stick the needle into the Humalog bottle.

3. Push the thumb plunger into the bottle so the air from the syringe goes in.
4. Draw up the 20 units; still draw slowly, making sure that the insulin is going in without air bubbles. If there are air bubbles, just push the insulin back into the syringe and try again.

Easy enough! This helps to ensure that you are getting the proper amount of insulin. I mention it here because we didn't learn this technique until Fred's sister, who is a nurse, told us this year. Fifteen years after we had been doing it incorrectly, thanks Mick!

Go to a nutritionist who can help you with better food choices. Reread the chapter on food. Don't make food a control issue/battle. Give them choices; explain, if possible, why it is important but then let them make at least some of their own decisions about the food they eat. Give them healthy options and make sure you are modeling that behavior! Don't get overwhelmed; do what you can!

LIFE BITES:

- Learn about your child's diagnosis so you have the information you need to make wise decisions.
- Keep learning as you go and figure out what works for you and make sure to be patient with yourself and other caregivers involved!
- Write down your emotions for 20 minutes, three days in a row. Learn how to feel emotions and let them go — good for our overall wellbeing.

THE BIG REVEAL

There is no one-size-fits-all approach to interacting with individuals with disabilities and being their parents. But the following interviews with individuals experiencing various types of disabilities offers us a one-size-fits-most approach. The questions that I posed to each interviewee were: What are the things your parents did that were most helpful? What do you wish they had done differently? How did your siblings feel? I hope you will find the information here to be useful tools that you can use in your role as a parent. I have added some commentary which I indicate by having it in parenthesis and italicized. These interviews have been incredibly revealing to me. I appreciate their willingness to share and their candor. I hope they will be revealing to you as well.

Richard—Richard is a friend whom I met through our Toastmaster's group, ToastAbility. Toastmaster's is an international organization that has been around for almost 100 years. The purpose is to improve individuals' speaking abilities and leadership skills. I chose to interview Richard because he does not let the fact that he is blind stop him from living life. Richard worked in the call center for the IRS for many years along with doing other types of work. Richard is blind because when he was 5 years old, doctors removed a tumor the size of a grapefruit that was growing inside of his brain. It was successfully removed, but it left him blind. He is working on his own book where you will be able to read the rest of his story. For now, this will be at least a glimpse into what has helped him become an amazing man.

To help Richard be successful, his parents sacrificed. When Richard was six years old, he went to live at a boarding school for the blind that was about 40 miles from his home. When he lived there, his dad would make sure to come to his dorm once a month late at night after a meeting he had been to in town. He would sit on the side of Richard's bed and talk about his own childhood and how Richard should behave, with words of wisdom like not to ever hit a woman. Because his father had made this time so special, Richard knew he should pay close attention to these words and put them into practice in his own life.

After Richard had lived there for a year, his family made the sacrifice to move from a four-bedroom house to a two-bedroom apartment for all six members of the family so that Richard could come home each night, allowing him to stay more connected to the family.

His father made sure to let Richard 'see' whatever he could, like he brought home wood that a beaver had gnawed so that Richard could feel it. One time, as they were driving along, his father noticed a bull elk standing close to the road on the other side of a fence. He pulled over and brought Richard to the great animal, so he could feel his antlers, which the elk graciously allowed him to do. His father made sure to include Richard in everything, even going with the other brothers each year to purchase a new car. Richard's brothers felt that Richard was the favorite kid because of the extra attention he received.

Richard wished that his parents had taught him more about being an adult, like about sex and financial management. They didn't teach him much about being an adult because the doctors had told them that Richard wouldn't live past 16 years old. They didn't tell him this until much later, but this shaped what they felt was necessary to teach him. It would have also been helpful if his parents had taught him more about cooking and cleaning, allowing him to try to do it even though it would have been challenging for him to learn. His mother did allow him to try to cook once, but he did something wrong and his mother immediately took everything out of his hands and would not let him try again. *(This is challenging for us parents to allow our kids to fail or do things below our standards, but as we will see in these interviews, it is important for our children's success that we give them these opportunities.)*

Richard also roller skated and rode bicycles as a kid. He could feel the vibration of the wall when he roller skated and he has a small bit of contrast vision which helped him determine where the wall was. When he rode his bike, he just stayed on the sidewalk. This was difficult when he rode in the shade but he still did it. These activities are things that his parents easily could have deemed 'too dangerous' for him to do but they didn't. They allowed him to do them, accepting the risk if he had failed. *(Isn't it interesting how some risks for our kids we can tolerate and some we can't — like cooking they couldn't tolerate, but riding a bike they could. I'm sure it has something to do with our own childhood and other factors. Use your own judgement as far as allowing your child to ride a bike, it is not safe for every child!)*

For Richard, friends were important. He is a social being and that has been another of his characteristics that has improved the quality of his life. His mother babysat ten children and he had three siblings, so he was always around people. His job growing up was to entertain the other kids and he helped with a Sunday school class. His Mom found these jobs that he could do and feel good about doing which were helpful in building his confidence. He has wonderful friends whom he has met from his church, our Toastmasters group, and other places. Richard is a singer and song writer. He writes many types of songs, including country and children's songs. He taught me about allowing our children to take risks even if that means they fail or fall, but they will also grow stronger and gain confidence.

Anna—Anna was an intern at Bayaud Enterprises. I chose to interview her because of her glowing confidence and willingness to participate in life, *all* of life. Little did I know that interviewing her would teach me so much! Anna has albinism, as does her sister. As a result of this lack of pigment, they are both legally blind; everything they see is blurry.

Anna has chosen, as an adult, to embrace her uniqueness. She is not afraid to stand out. She decided to use a cane for a couple of reasons. One reason was to be able to navigate her surroundings more safely. The other was to acknowledge her blindness so that people are usually more kind when she asks for help although there are times that because of the cane, people give her too much help. She has learned to accept that, too. It is always best to first ask someone if they want help before you just grab their elbow and take them where you believe they want to go!

There are three primary factors that her parents did that Anna credits for her success as an adult. The first is the fact that her sister has the same condition. Even though they approach their challenges differently, they are very close because of the genes they share. Anna's sister has focused on using her vision to the best of her abilities. In Anna's opinion, this is hard work and straining on the eyes. This is a more common approach in the community of those who have albinism. Anna has embraced her blindness and accepts the accommodations she needs, which has served her well. She doesn't feel the strain of trying to see and not stand out. She accepts all of who she is, accepting help and accommodations so that she can experience the fullness of the world around her.

Secondly, her parents allowed them to do things on their own. They even made the decision when Anna was 10 years old to move to Boulder, Colorado, because it had a good bus system. They have parents who thought ahead and moved to a place where they knew the girls could experience more independence because of a bus system that allowed for increased mobility.

The third factor, that assisted Anna with becoming such an amazing young woman, was her parents' decision to put her in a small, private school for grades K through 12 called the Waldorf School in Boulder. This school didn't know a great deal about how to accommodate someone with disabilities, but it did know how to celebrate each student's abilities, listen to their needs, and develop their strengths. In this small environment, Anna wasn't teased or bullied. She was just allowed to be her own unique self, as were her fellow classmates. This encouragement and love of learning has taken her far!

Here are Anna's insights in her own words:

"One of the things that I appreciate about my own upbringing is that my parents didn't define my disability for me. They didn't ignore or try to hide or fix my blindness. They also didn't go overboard trying to get me all the right gadgets, and training, and supports, to be a successful blind person as defined by the blindness advocacy organizations or society. What they did do, to the best of their abilities, was educate themselves on options, and then pass those options along to me in the form of choices. Of course, when I was little, they used parental authority to make lots of decisions — like what glasses I would wear, what school I would attend, how many minutes I could be in the sun before covering up or wearing sunscreen, etc. But as soon as I was old enough to articulate what worked well for me and what didn't, they listened.

They tried hard to protect me and equip me to be successful, but they didn't define what "success" looks like. They taught me that my perceptions of and ways of being in the world are unique and worthy. Beyond this, they trusted me to make of my life what I will. Because of this upbringing, when I later discovered and became involved with blind and disabled communities and embraced my identity as a blind/disabled person, taking on these labels and identities was empowering for me because I chose them. I hadn't been taught that I was blind, or that it should look like this or that, or that I was sighted and should hide my vision problems. I was taught simply that my ways of being in the world are unique and that one dimension of my uniqueness is my albinism.

I'm grateful for this upbringing. I think it's served me well."

Anna's parents allowed her to travel to India when she was just 19 years old. She has also been there five other times. While she was there, she visited a school for the blind. They asked her to speak to a class of girls. As she spoke to the group, the lights went out. No one reacted at all. This was such a moment of awakening and connection for Anna.

She also took classes at Gallaudet University which is a university for individuals who are deaf and hard of hearing. Anna used a sign interpreter to sign to her what was going on in the room around her instead of what was being said. She would feel the person's hands as they signed to her. This allowed her to get the full experience of the class and everyone in it. She revealed to me that in that moment, she felt the least disabled she had ever felt. It was in allowing herself to acknowledge all the things her body couldn't do, and accept the help to do it, that she felt the least disabled! *(Wow! We work so hard to make our children fit in when perhaps what we should be doing is allowing them to accept and love all of who they are — even the parts that aren't easy to accept.)*

Katy— Katy is our middle child. I chose to interview her because of her zest for life, her ability to work hard, overcome barriers, and live courageously. She has life threatening allergies, endometriosis, rheumatoid arthritis, and some cognitive processing issues. She is also one of the editors of this book — another one of her skills.

Katy is grateful that she learned how to be strong, take care of a house, and cook. Life was never easy but usually fun and an adventure. She also was taught that everyone has something to add to the world and no one is all bad, so you might as well make friends with everyone. She learned how to have a house that you are proud of and most of all, that no matter what goes on in life, it can't be done alone.

She was shown that the world is not a scary place but a place of adventure and fun. Sometimes it is hard, but you must just breathe and get through it. Even when life got hard, and she did not know if she was going to make it, her parents stood by her side and had a positive attitude. All the things that the family has been through has created a strong bond between them.

From her father, she learned that passion is important and to never give up and that race cars can be the most exciting thing in the world. Sometimes the strongest people are the last people you think of and she learned the importance of humility.

Knowing that her parents loved her was an important piece of her becoming the woman she is today. One of the other things that helped was that Katy went to Rocky Mountain School of Expeditionary Learning which really developed in her a deep love of learning and taught her how to challenge herself. She went there from first grade to her high school graduation. *(I am grateful for how much this school helped Katy to really find herself. Alli also went to this school, but just for her four years of high school. It helped her tremendously, too).*

It was difficult being a sibling, let alone a twin, to a brother with Down syndrome. Attention was something that was in short supply because of this. Her mom and dad tried to spend one on one time with each child, but there were times that was not possible. She is grateful for the attention her grandmother was able to give her. From the time Katy was about ten years old, her grandmother would take her each summer on a little vacation. This was a special time for them and a time without the distraction of her brother — when she could just get beautiful attention from her beloved grandmother. She would also have Katy over to spend the night or just hang out for a while. They still have a close relationship, for which they are both grateful. The more people in your life who love you, the better!

It would have been helpful if after her big sister Alli moved out of the house that they would have spent more time together. *(After Alli moved out, we didn't see her much. She was living with a man who was controlling and it was not a good situation. She moved back home after about nine years when Katy had already moved away..)*

She wished that after traumatic incidents with Alex that we would have debriefed to help work through all the fear and emotions we were all feeling — really talk about what happened, make sure we realized it is nobody's 'fault', forgive ourselves, each other, and Alex for what occurred and let it go.

Because Katy lives in pain most of the time, it is not helpful to ask her every day, "How are you?" It can make the person feel like they need to say, "I'm fine," even when she isn't. It may be more helpful to be aware if she seems to be having a hard day, take extra time to be with her, or offer to do some things for her, like open a jar, which is difficult because of the arthritis, but *not* baby her. It can be a fine line between the two. Just take the time to be aware and sense how they are and allow them to have the best day possible.

And she wished we had been more active as a family, like working out, going for walks, etc. We are definitely *not* an athletic or active family by nature, but it would have been helpful for all of us to just incorporate movement more into our lives.

Elayna—Elayna worked in the marketing department of Bayaud Enterprises. I chose to interview her because of her creativity, knowledge of marketing, her positive attitude and passion for life. What I learned from interviewing her is how much kids can endure and how it builds strong character and determination.

Elayna was born with Pseudarthrosis which is a congenital bone disease where the body tries to form a false joint after a fracture. This is such a rare condition; she has only met one other person with it. Because of this condition, she has been through many surgeries in her life. As a result, she grew up on crutches and was in a body cast a couple times when she was three and four years old.

Because of a courageous doctor named Dr. Dror Palley, some of the surgeries she had were to attach an ilizarov device which is used to lengthen and reshape bones. It is basically an external fixator that is made up of pins that go through the bone and come out the other side and attach to rings that typically surrounds the leg. She had this device on from age eight to ten, and again at age 15. Her mom would make covers out of pillowcases to cover the device and keep it clean. As a child, she would climb trees when she had it on. She has a high pain tolerance; she even had them change a pin once without anesthesia!

Her parents didn't treat her like she was super special and they didn't spoil her. She is grateful she was not babied. 'Disability' was not a word in her house growing up and she didn't realize she was disabled until she was much older. After one of Elayna's major surgeries, she had to use a different doctor. This doctor insisted that she be on pain medications which she hadn't been given after previous surgeries. She had a bad reaction to the meds which gave her hallucinations and other unwanted reactions. Elayna was finally able to convince her mom that it was the drugs causing the visions and they were not her imagination! This gave her mom the strength to stand up to the doctor and tell him to stop giving her the pain medications. Her mother is typically shy and not comfortable standing up for her daughter *(definitely an issue for me as well)*. But by the end of this surgery with a new doctor, she was more able to stand up to the doctors and other professionals for the sake of her daughter.

Elayna has learned through all her interactions with medical professionals that doctors should listen to patients and their parents because they really do know their own body or that of their child and how they're feeling. Elayna and her parents have all learned that the first answer from a doctor is not always the right answer and that all doctors are not created equally! It is important to find a doctor who cares, takes the time to really listen, and is at least a bit humble.

With all the travel to doctors who lived in various parts of the country, her parents had to sacrifice, learn how to advocate, and get creative with resolving the issues of having a child in such a cumbersome device. Her father used his problem-solving skills to make her a skateboard type device that she could lay on and pull herself around when she was young and in a full body cast.

The question of what her parents could have done differently was a difficult question to answer because Elayna, like the others I have interviewed, realized that their parents did the best they could with the knowledge they had at the time. A couple of things that in hindsight might have been helpful were to have her included in the medical decisions at an earlier age — at least so she could understand more of why they made the choices they did regarding her health and she could have voiced her own concerns. If they had done this, it is possible they would have decided to amputate her leg which may have resulted in living with less pain for her as an adult. (*Elayna has since had her leg amputated which has alleviated some pain but it has been a big adjustment for her*).

Elayna's family is one who doesn't really talk about emotions, which is the way many families are, but children need a safe place to express their emotions. At some point, Elayna began seeing a therapist for depression. When she shared this with her mom, she tried to diminish the diagnosis instead of acknowledging it. Perhaps it would have been more helpful if her parents had talked to her about it and helped her process it — also allowed her to see the therapist more so that she could have learned to have a deeper understanding of how she was feeling and learn some coping mechanisms. (*This is important for our children and families to help them deal in a healthy way with all of the emotions and issues that are a part of life for each one of us. We needed to go to family and individual counseling which was helpful in dealing with many of the issues we had because we were part of the Drake family. Unfortunately, we still deal with the stigma of any mental health issue which keeps many people from seeking the help that we all need from time to time in our lives*).

Elayna's siblings are quite a bit older than she is which distanced them a little from what was happening. Her parents treated her, as much as possible, like they did her other siblings. They, again, didn't really talk about the issues that this probably brought up.

Another situation Elayna deals with because she doesn't present as having any disabilities, except that she walks with a slight limp, is people seldom believe she needs any accommodations. She does have a placard for her car, but when she uses it, she almost feels like she needs to exaggerate her limp to justify it to others. This can be a common issue for those who have invisible disabilities. Walking down an airplane aisle is quite painful for her because of the angle of the walkway and her ankle's inability to move that way, but she doesn't always feel like asking to go on first because of it. She feels judgment from others about her level of disability. She has had people comment to her when she parks in a handicapped parking space even though she has the placard, so sometimes she just avoids it and walks farther. If someone has a placard on their car and they are in a handicapped spot, let that be enough for your curiosity and don't worry about why they need it.

She is grateful to the amazing doctors she had who were willing to take risks and help her. She is grateful to her parents who found those doctors, and who made sure she had access to them. Her journey has created in her a sense of determination that has, and will, carry her far.

Joe—Joe is one of the founding members of our Toastmaster's group, ToastAbility. I chose to interview Joe for his many accomplishments. He was the first blind juror in Denver. The case he sat on was a highly publicized murder trial. He proved that it was possible. He is also a competitive ballroom dancer with beautiful moves and one of the most knowledgeable people that I know about the history of our country. Joe had been blind since birth in his left eye, but then at age eight, he lost sight in his right eye due to a detached retina and glaucoma. He was also diagnosed as being bipolar when he was in his early 30's.

Joe credits his success to his mother who loved, supported him, and believed in him. Joe is grateful that his mother let him try to do things on his own, within reason. She let him ride a bike; he had a three-wheeler so that he didn't have to balance. He could ride a two-wheeler but it was more difficult. Joe also got to drive a car. He sat on his dad's lap and helped drive. There was another time when a friend of his mother's who was a driving instructor allowed him to drive the student car around a parking lot. It would have been interesting if the people in the parking lot that day had known Joe was blind!

Joe's mother was married six times. Each one of his dads taught him something. Because of this, he has a knowledge of construction, carpentry, how to work on cars, how oil rigs work, etc. It has also given him some funny topics for his speeches at ToastAbility!

He was mainstreamed for school which worked well for him. He is quite intelligent and social so he was successful at school. He had friends but did experience some teasing, just like many people.

The question of what could have been done differently was also difficult for Joe to answer. But because of all the marriages, there were times that weren't really stable. His mother did the best she could to make sure that their home was as stable and full of love as possible. One thing he did say was that getting the mental health diagnosis as early as possible and being open to treatment are paramount for a healthy outcome. We, as a society, need to let go of the stigma of mental health so that people are encouraged to get the help they need when they need it most, which is in the early stages of the diagnosis.

Joe has a sister but doesn't remember her having any issues because of his blindness. She got things because she was sighted, like a car when she was 16, and he got some extra attention because of the blindness. It was what it was. They were also close because they were together through all the marriages.

Catherine—Catherine, aside from being one of my best friends, is one of my favorite people to have deep discussions with. She is capable, courageous, compassionate, and a loyal friend who has overcome great obstacles while keeping a positive attitude. Catherine has attention deficit hyperactivity disorder — ADHD.

Her parents always encouraged her feelings of compassion for people and animals. One time, when she was in kindergarten, which was in the 50's, there were Pyracantha berries outside the fence on the playground of the school. The birds would come and eat the berries, get drunk, then fly into the windows of the school which killed them. It was so upsetting to the young Catherine that she would dig a little hole in the playground, bury each bird, and make a little cross to mark each grave. She created hundreds of these little graves for the bird victims. Her teacher called her parents and told them that there was something wrong with their daughter. Her mother replied that it wasn't Catherine who had the problem, but the teacher. She then suggested that the teacher read about Mother Theresa.

Catherine's deep sense of compassion, which would make her cry when she would watch movies like Old Yeller, led her to begin her own non-profit as an adult. The mission of her non-profit was to find people who would adopt the children of parents dying of AIDS before the person passed so they would know that their children would be well cared for. The encouragement she received from her parents led her on a pathway to her own success.

Another encouragement she received was from her father who believed strongly in her skills as a swimmer. When she was 14 years old, her father called George Haines, who was the coach for the Olympics swim team and lived about ten miles from where they lived. He asked Coach Haines to give his daughter a chance to work with him. The coach agreed to a meeting. He told Catherine to swim in the lap pool. She was a bundle of nerves, but she did it. When she got out of the pool, Coach Haines just looked at her dad and said, "She's on the team." This was a turning point in her life. She knew she was gifted and there was something she could do really well. It kept her from thinking she was stupid, gave her a great work ethic, and taught her to be disciplined.

Because of this, she went to college. School had always been difficult for her but she persevered and after seven years, she had a three-year degree in interior design with a 4.0 grade point average and a bachelor's degree in social work.

She really wished her parents had taught her life skills, like cleaning her room, doing her laundry, cooking, and everything else. They did not take seriously how much the ADHD affected her life. When she was in school, she seldom understood what her teacher was saying. She didn't learn much at all. She went to a finishing school in California where she learned how to set a great table and entertain. This knowledge was not helpful when she got to college.

Her parents did not have her do any chores or work at all around the house. They had help that did those kinds of things. She never even babysat in her youth. She was given any material thing she wanted. When she was a teenager, she had a huge ego because of her ability to swim and the fact that she got whatever she wanted and didn't have to work for any of it. This did not serve her well years later when she would be challenged with homelessness in her 60's. She was not taught how to handle money at all. It would have been helpful for her parents to give her chores to do where she could earn money which she would have been responsible for spending. This would have taught her more about the value of money.

Erica—Erica is another Bayaud Enterprises employee whom I chose because of her ability to do her job with so much heart for those she serves. She began at Bayaud, assisting clients with finding the services they need and for which they qualify, like food assistance, Medicaid, low-income housing, as well as other critical services. Then she earned her master's degree in social work. She is now licensed and works as a counselor for Bayaud clients.

Erica was born with cerebral palsy which affected her mobility. Then when she was 12 years old, she was in a skiing accident that resulted in a traumatic brain injury (TBI). This further decreased her balance, making her more reliant on a wheelchair.

The best thing her parents did was to unconditionally love her and believe in her. Her mother, Joy, has been the strongest influence on Erica. She has been the constant in her life. Her mom attended all of her IEP's, bringing an advocate if necessary, and made sure she had any accommodations she needed. Erica has a younger sister. Joy held both of them to the same standards as much as possible. They each had chores for which they were responsible and they were required to do their best academically. Even though her mom was always around, she let Erica do things on her own.

One time, when Erica was in middle school, she was failing a typing class. Her mom got pressure from other parents to step in to make sure her daughter didn't fail. But after she spoke with Erica's teacher, she felt that the teacher was being reasonable, so she stepped back and let Erica receive natural consequences for her choices. Erica began working harder in the class. She ended up passing the class because she learned how to type. This skill has served her well as it has allowed her to use the computer for school, work, and life.

Without her typing ability, she would not be able to do her current job and she wouldn't be able to make a difference in the lives of individuals challenged with homelessness like she does. Let me say that again, if her mother had taken away her struggle and made the teacher pass Erica, she would not have learned to type, which has enabled her to work at Bayaud and make a difference in the lives of many people. Struggle can be a wonderful teacher and help us build strength.

The skiing injury happened when Erica was 12 years old. As I mentioned, it caused a TBI that changed her ability to function as she had before; it honestly almost *killed* her. Even though this had happened, Erica wanted to ski again, and her parents let her! That takes courageous parenting. Here is what that decision taught Erica:

- Fear doesn't have to stop her.
- Sometimes it is the difficult moments in life that foster deep, lasting relationships (she became close friends with her ski instructor).
- She could face huge challenges head on and persevere through them, like completing college.

It would have been so much easier at the time to stop skiing, but easier is not always better!

Joy made other sacrifices for Erica's success. She was, for the most part, a single mom. Erica had many surgeries which impacted her mother's ability to work. There were times when she could only work part time or not at all. They had to occasionally be on public assistance, like food assistance, but they made the most of it. Having a child with a disability can make life more challenging but it also has the potential to create a powerful bond between the members of the family. Joy always put her children's needs first; she made them a priority. There is a great deal of trust and love in the family.

Another important activity that Erica, her sister, and mother did was to volunteer. They volunteered at Children's Hospital which allowed them to give back to the hospital that had helped Erica with her CP and heal after her accident. It developed confidence in her ability to make a difference in the world and let her know that she could work.

Erica went to public school in Lakewood, Colorado. During high school, she had several surgeries which meant that she missed two to three semesters and needed tutors to complete her studies. Joy advocated during her high school years to make sure that Erica got the academic classes she would need so that she could fulfill her dream to be the first in her family to go to college. Erica had a vocational rehabilitation counselor who didn't believe she could go to college. But Erica proved him wrong by not only graduating from college, but also receiving a Daniel's Fund scholarship to do so and going on to earn her master's degree.

Joy taught her that if you want something to go for it and that 'no' is not always the final answer. She also taught Erica coping skills, that it is okay to cry. It is important to let emotions out. She taught her how to solve problems, to figure things out, look for solutions, and to determine how to allow yourself to feel your emotions and use them in ways that lead to success as opposed to making situations worse. (*There is a great book on this topic called Emotional Agility by Susan David Ph.d.*)

During Erica's childhood, she required various types of therapies which meant Erica and her mother would go to these therapies often without her little sister. Joy felt like this was unfair to the sister so she would take her places so they could spend time alone. As a child, this didn't feel fair to Erica since she was at therapy appointments, not having fun which is what her sister and her mom were doing. In the end, Erica and Joy worked through the disagreement by communicating and spending time doing fun things as a family. Ultimately, it's not only the amount of time you spend with loved ones, but also the *quality* of that time. Sure, take care of what needs to be done but make time to just be together without distractions —even cell phones!

Erica and her partner have a son and a daughter. There were people who told Erica that she couldn't be a mom or wouldn't be a good mom. But Erica's mom believed in her ability to do this important job. Joy is good at allowing Erica to be a mom but she also sees when she needs a break which is incredibly helpful! They have worked out boundaries that are healthy and work for grandmother, mother, and child.

Bullying wasn't something that Erica has experienced much of but not being included happened all the time. She was not invited to parties or other events. It is hard to tell what a parent can do to help with this, except to create the events themselves.

As with most mothers, one thing that would have been helpful to see modeled more is Erica's mom allowing herself time for more self-care. This is a challenge for us mothers but if we did allow ourselves this time, it would not only help us, it would be good for our children as well. Possibly taking a long bath before bed, finding a quiet place to read a book, and having a wet washcloth beside you so if your child does come up wanting something, you can wash their face first *(this is an idea from someone else, but it sounded pretty good to me)!* Simple things can give us a small break in our day and provide us with a little self care.

Erica's sister provides a great source of love and support to her. When she thinks of her sister, she sees her as her advocate and friend. They have a deep love for their nieces and nephews and they know they would do anything for each other. Her sister cares about disability issues and being an advocate for all people. They live about eight hours away from each other and even though they speak weekly, the separation is still hard for both of them and their children. Their close relationship is an important piece of both of their lives and the lives of their children.

Alli—Alli, our oldest daughter, has worked for an ambulance company for fourteen years. She started as a receptionist, then was promoted to billing and coding and was recently promoted to a lead position. She is a leader in two Toastmasters groups and participates in her community. She speaks fluent Spanish and conversational American Sign Language. I chose to interview Alli, who has ADD and dyslexia, because of all she has accomplished and the compassionate person she has become.

School was exceedingly difficult for Alli but she was very glad her parents let her struggle on her own and learn in her own way. She is also glad that her parents were always ready to help her when she needed it. When it got too hard, they would try to find other methods of teaching (tutoring etc.) which also helped. The focus was not on her learning disability but on her.

Sometimes being the sibling of someone with a disability (her brother with Down syndrome and sister with severe allergies), there are times you feel ignored. She wished she had more time alone with just her parents. Having dyslexia — sometimes you feel like the odd person out, so it would have been nice to find a group of other people who had the same issues so as not to feel quite as alone.

It is hard to have a sibling with a disability; she is glad her family always stayed together and helped each other when needed. It is important to educate all siblings that they are valued for who they are. Make sure if you lean on one sibling more, to try to compensate them in some way for the help they provide; it can make them feel needed and show them responsibility can be beneficial. *(From the time Alli was 13 years old until she left home at 19, she was responsible for watching Alex and Katy when they got home from school until Fred or I got home. Because we didn't have much money at the time, not only were we unable to pay her, but she also couldn't get a job somewhere else because we needed her at home. It was not fair to her and we obviously could have handled it better.)*

There are times when people stare at individuals who have disabilities which is hard on the siblings who often see this. It would be helpful to find ways to deal with staring, like perhaps educating people or finding ways to ignore them and just give the sibling with disabilities all the love that they deserve so that they don't care that people stare at them. Learning to love ourselves improves all areas of our lives and the lives of those around us.

Final thoughts—Sometimes, as parents of children with various disabilities or medical conditions, we get asked how we do it. As these interviews illustrate, we do our best with the information we have. We get up in the morning and face the challenges and the joys of that day. We hear a new diagnosis, so we read about it; we google it; we learn what we need to know to make the best of it, like any parent would. We learn how to make pieces of clothing out of pillowcases to hide our child's medical device; we figure out what cities have the best bus system to give our kids the best chance at independence; we create stability through six marriages; we take our kids to feel what they can so they can 'see' the world; we learn whatever we need to get us through the day. When night comes, we lay our heads down and sleep so that we can get up and do it again tomorrow.

These interviews were eye-opening for me. They taught me so much about what is important. I hope they have helped you as well! And remember, the purpose of parenting is not to be perfect, but rather to be a loving parent who finds the lessons of life and learns to laugh and let go!

LIFE BITES:

- We see how important it is to love our children, to let them know they matter, to embrace all of who we are and teach our children to do the same.
- Know the value of allowing ourselves and our children the opportunity to fail, to know that we can get back up and try

again and, more importantly, to learn from those failures.
- We have learned that struggle can be a powerful teacher, forging in us the steel of character and determination that take us far in life.
- Take time to listen, really listen to those we love and spend quality time together.
- We find the joy, the laughter, the hope, and the sorrow that the day brings. Hopefully we learn the lessons, the beautiful lessons that few others have the opportunity to have so readily available.
- We use these lessons, this knowledge, to not only become our best selves, but also to guide our children to do the same.
- Embrace the power of imperfect parenting and in doing so, you will find it really is all perfect.

ABOUT THE AUTHOR

Lynda Drake worked for Bayaud Enterprises from 2006 to 2022 as a job developer and program manager. She has assisted over a thousand individuals in their job search as well as facilitating Beyond Bayaud for 15 years, which was a class where she strived to give people the tools necessary to rise above poverty and find their own personal power to create the life they desire and deserve. Before coming to Bayaud, she had been a stockbroker for Ameritrade and Charles Schwab for 19 years. Having children with various disabilities led her to work in the non-profit world where she has found fulfillment and an ability to truly connect to others.

She and her late husband have three children. They are all powerfully imperfect people who each have their own challenges: their oldest daughter, Alli, and twins, a son, Alex and daughter, Katy.

Lynda has written two books, one about money from a spiritual point of view called, *Belly Dancing Lessons for Your Finances, a Spiritual Guide to Financial Health* and *The Power of Imperfect Parents*, about parenting children with special needs. Lynda is also a life coach, professional speaker, and group facilitator. If you are interested in having her speak at an event, please contact her at Lyndadrake@protonmail.com.

ABOUT THE ORIGINAL COVER ARTIST

Johnene Tung lives in Denver, CO. She is 32 and last year in 2017 she lost both legs and her left arm to a bone infection. She has always been an artist. Johnene graduated from a trade school where she learned graphic design then studied photography at the Art Institute and all the while, she painted in her spare time. Life as a triple amputee hasn't been easy. Things she did without even having to think are now impossible and finding work isn't much more likely. It is people like Lynda that see past a person's disabilities to what they're truly capable of that give her hope and the confidence to keep trying. You can reach her at **johnenet33@gmail.com.**

SAYINGS FOR LIFE

This too shall pass! Mickie Stackhouse

Look at everything that happens in life as if you had chosen it; work with it, don't fight it. Eckhart Tolle

I am enough! Marisa Peer

I let go of all negative emotions; I will not resist my life, but I will let my life flow, joyously and freely. Lynda Drake

Blessings for your child—"I send you blessings of love and health, abundance well used and whatever is in your highest good is what will happen. I send you blessings that your voice is heard and your talents are shared in ways that make the world be a better place. Blessings that you learn what you are here to learn and that my heart and mind are open in ways to guide you on your path and to learn from you the lessons you are here to give me."

Blessings for professionals—"I send you blessings of gratitude that you are in your right job, that you live in integrity and compassion, and blessings of gratitude for your wisdom in guiding my child in health or learning and your courage to be innovative and wise."

Sing "Hu" which is an ancient word for God. This is sung on middle C for as long as you can; take breaths as needed. This helps to improve the vibration or positive energy in the situation.

What you focus on, you will get more of — make sure you are focusing on what you want!

Remember to love yourself. You are worthy of this important job you have been chosen to do. Don't be hard on yourself; just do your best, then when the day is done, go to sleep. Tomorrow you will wake up and have a chance to do it again, maybe just a little bit better than you did yesterday!

Here is some final wisdom from Emily Perl Kingley, author of the poem *Welcome to Holland* and mother of a son with Down syndrome:

"I think I'd say "take it easy, catch your breath, meet a bunch of other families, other children, don't worry, it's going to be okay. This is the same child you would have had anyway, with all the things he or she would have inherited from you and your husband, take one step at a time, have fun, learn, laugh, love, cry, whatever you **feel,** it'll be okay. Find some other moms who are going down this road with you. Your baby will teach you the way. Lots of hugging, lots of singing, then lots more hugging."

Books Mentioned:

Four Reincarnations by Max Ritvo
The Gentle Art of Blessing by Pierre Pradervand
The Gift of Dyslexia by Ronald D. Davis
Conversations with God by Neal Donald Walsch
Me to We by Craig Kielburger

www.ingramcontent.com/pod-product-compliance
Lightning Source LLC
LaVergne TN
LVHW011951070526
838202LV00054B/4892